Williams RENAULT
FORMULA 1
MOTOR RACING BOOK

INTRODUCTION BY ALAIN PROST

DK

DORLING KINDERSLEY
LONDON • NEW YORK • STUTTGART

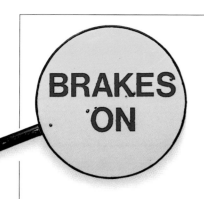

BRAKES ON

A DORLING KINDERSLEY BOOK
Commissioned and conceived by RENAULT
Designed and illustrated by DORLING KINDERSLEY
Written by XAVIER CHIMITS AND FRANÇOIS GRANET

Project Director: *Peter Bridgewater*
Designers: *Peter Bridgewater and Terry Jeavons*
Photography: *Guy Ryecart*
Models: *Mark Jamieson*
Typesetter: *Vanessa Good*
Editor: *Ian Whitelaw*
Illustrations: *Andrew Milne*
Art Director: *Stuart Jackman, Dorling Kindersley*
Translation: *Chris Williams*

ACKNOWLEDGMENTS
Paul Belmondo, Eric Bernard, Eric Bhat, Alexandrine Breton,
François Chaignon, Pierre Dupasquier, Jean-Claude Fayard,
Damon Hill, Dany Hindenoch, Philippe Leloup,
Jo Ramirez, Chris Staveley, Michel Têtu, Dan Tréma, Arai, Bell,
Carbone Industrie, Elf, FIA, Goodyear,
IBSV/Rhône-Poulenc, Renault-Sport, Stand 21, Williams.

Some of the technical details in this book were taken from
"Conduite en compétition", by Pierre-François Rousselot and
Alain Prost, Editions Robert Laffont.

Picture credits
ALLSPORT p. 7, 13, 15-20, 22, 24, 25, 27-30, 32, 33, 38, 40-48, 53, 54,
56, 57, 59, 60, 62, 63. AUTOMEDIA p. 6, 15. AUTOPRESSE p. 9, 49-
51, 56-59, 63. BEAULIEU p. 12, 15, 16, 30, 57, 58, 59.
D.P.P.I. p. 8, 11, 14, 15, 17, 21, 24, 29, 32, 36, 39, 41, 42, 44, 45, 49,
57, 61-63, end papers. L.A.T. p. 8, 58, 63. MARY EVANS p. 16.
PHOTOTHÈQUE RENAULT p. 6, 9, 11, 12, 16, 18, 19, 27,41, 45.
GUY RYECART p. 6-17, 19-28, 30, 31, 33-56, 59-63.
STEVE SWOPE RACING PHOTOS p. 49. PETER TEMPEST p. 14.
WAKE UPP p. 26, 48.

First published in Great Britain in 1994 by
Dorling Kindersley Limited, 9 Henrietta Street, London WC2E 8PS

A CIP catalogue record for this book is available
from the British Library

ISBN 0 7513 0109 4

Printed and bound in Italy by New Interlitho, Milan

Contents

Preface

I have read many books on the subject of Formula 1 and I thought there was nothing left to write.

Not so.

The Williams-Renault Formula 1 Book, through both its contents and presentation, offers a thoroughly fresh vision of the sport.

Look as you might, you won't come across any review of the last season in its pages. Nor will you discover any sort of analysis of the strengths and weaknesses of individual teams, nor biographies of those drivers who have marked Formula 1 over the years.

For this book is totally different – a genuine in-depth guide to what goes on behind the scenes, delving into a universe, my universe, which only a select few can truly claim to know. Even many of those directly involved in the sport – drivers,

team managers, engineers, officials and journalists – do not have such a broad grasp of day-to-day life in Formula 1.

This book explores all the aspects that neither television commentators nor journalists, absorbed as they are by the race itself, have time to cover... a thousand and one fascinating details – sometimes amusing, often surprising – that make Formula 1 a world apart. A world constantly in the limelight, yet which harbours so many secrets. Big and small.

Without a doubt, this original work answers all the questions I am so often asked by Formula 1 fans – even by F1 buffs – who are looking for a more detailed understanding of the world of Formula 1.

A Formula 1 car is born

THE BIRTH OF A FORMULA 1 CAR is a long and complex affair, and up to six months are required from the initial sketches to the first track tests. Computers play a key role in this process and, thanks to simulation software, engineers are able to evaluate the car's potential in advance. However, in ultra-modern factories like those of Williams and McLaren who produce in-house some 90% of the parts they use, machines have not yet replaced human skills entirely. There is still no robot, for example, able to shape exhaust pipes to make them hug the contours of the engine.

SIMULATED SPEED
Before a car is built, scale models are tested in a wind tunnel. Winds of up to 300 kilometres per hour (kph) simulate the sort of speeds the car will reach on the track.

THE COMPOSITES SPECIALIST
Honeycomb structures and materials such as carbon, "Kevlar", fibre-glass and resin used in the making of the chassis hold no secrets for the composite laminator

Aluminium honeycomb

Carbon sheet

ALUMINIUM SANDWICH
To build the tub, composite materials specialists bond an aluminium honeycomb between two sheets of carbon. This is then polymerised in a vacuum oven. The result is twice as light and twice as strong as aluminium.

THE DRAUGHTSMAN
It is the draughtsman who either draws up the parts to be used on the car or else translates engineers' requirements into computer language. In some teams, it is the engineers themselves who carry out this work

THE TECHNICAL DIRECTOR
He is essentially the project leader, the person who takes all the technical decisions, who coordinates the work of his engineers and who supervises the development of the car on the track

"Nomex" honeycomb is even lighter than its aluminium equivalent

"NOMEX" HONEYCOMB
"Nomex" honeycomb is used for the narrower parts of the tub such as the nose cone. Whilst not quite so rigid as aluminium, it is lighter, more flexible and easier to work.

MASTERMINDS OF PERFORMANCE
Between them, these nine men represent the different trades involved in creating a Formula 1 car. Highly-qualified engineers and technicians work under the orders of the team's technical director who can be described as the true 'father' of the car.
The increasing use of complex technology has led teams to recruit their engineers directly from leading technical and aeronautical colleges.

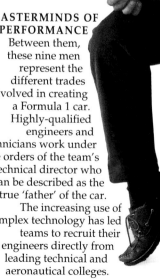

SIX STAGES IN THE BUILDING OF A FORMULA 1 CAR

STAGE 1
Before being painted, the tub, which is made from laminated carbon sheets, is baked in a vacuum oven

STAGE 2
Side pods on either side of the tub house the radiators that cool the engine

STAGE 3
The engine is rigidly mounted to the rear of the tub

STAGE 4
The gearbox, once assembled (20 hours' work), is coupled to the engine

STAGE 5
Wishbones, suspension, brakes and rear running-gear are added

STAGE 6
The wings, bodywork and wheels are fitted. The car is finally mobile. Only the electronic management of the gearbox, engine and, in certain cases, suspension remains to be programmed before the car is ready to drive

THE ELECTRONICS SPECIALIST
Responsible for the development and supervision of all electrical and electronic systems used on the car

MACHINISTS
Turners, millers and fitters use computer-controlled machine tools to manufacture the parts designed by the engineers

THE MECHANIC
He is the person who assembles the car once all the parts are ready. He might also work on the car at the track

PAINTWORK AND DECORATION
Once painting of the car has been completed, decals are applied to those places agreed with sponsors

DESIGN ENGINEER
The design engineer is responsible for quality control of parts and he supervises the assembly of the car. He might also attend the car's maiden track test before it passes into the hands of the race-team

AERO-DYNAMICS ENGINEER
Responsible for the shape of the car, the aerodynamics engineer spends much of his time in the wind-tunnel, where he tests all new body parts and designs the wings

Rules and regulations

Since its creation in 1950, the World Championship has undergone numerous regulation changes. For reasons of safety, the governing body has periodically sought to channel the ingenuity of engineers whose prime objective is always to improve the performance of their machine. In just over twenty pages, the championship's technical regulations clearly set out the limits within which engineers can work. A quick read reveals that a Formula 1 car is defined as "a vehicle running on at least four non-aligned complete wheels, of which at least two are for steering and at least two for propulsion". Given the lengths that designers will go to in order to gain those all important hundredths of a second, this basic definition is extremely necessary.

SAFETY FUEL TANK
Fuel tanks must be deformable and puncture-proof. The 'bladders' are made from rubber reinforced with "Kevlar", and fuel pipes from the tank must be of the automatic cut-off type

REMOVABLE STEERING WHEEL
In order to allow drivers to climb swiftly out of the cockpit, steering wheels must be fitted with a quick-release system

NOSE-CONE
The distance between the front of the car and the centre-line of the front axle may not exceed 120 cm. Width is restricted to 140 cm

IMPACT-ABSORBING BODY
Like road cars, an example of every new Formula 1 car is subjected to a crash-test

SLIM-LINE
The minimum overall weight of a Formula 1 car is 505 kg. There is no length restriction, although maximum values have been set for front and rear overhang. Width must not exceed 200 cm and overall height must be no more than 100 cm. All parts used in the car's construction are governed by their own specific regulations.

DUAL-CIRCUIT BRAKES
The braking system is divided into two independent circuits. In the event of a problem with one, the other continues to function

FOUR WHEELS
A Formula 1 car must have four wheels, the width of which may not exceed 15 in. Bodywork must not cover the wheels

EXPLOITING THE REGULATIONS

F1 is an ongoing combat between legislators and engineers, the former seeking to curb the creative instinct of the latter. Indeed, the task of the sport's governing body is to ensure that F1 cars stay within reasonable limits. For example, aerofoil brakes (1968), the use of 6-wheels (1976) or 'fan-cars' (1978) were all outlawed. Had they not been, safety might have taken a step backwards whilst spectator interest would have gained nothing.

Rear of the Brabham
BT 46 B 'fan-car' (1978)

Tyrrell P34
6-wheeler (1976)

THE LEGISLATORS

The fourteen members of the Technical Commission are elected by the World Council, the highest authority of the Fédération Internationale de l'Automobile (FIA). These highly-qualified technicians and engineers, one of whom represents the teams, prepare the regulations, which are subsequently submitted to the World Council for approval.

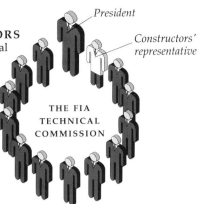

President

Constructors' representative

THE FIA TECHNICAL COMMISSION

THE 1950s
With front-mounted engines, chassis rails, 'cigar' aerodynamics, narrow wheels, and drivers sitting in the upright position, cars in Formula 1's heroic days were similar in design to pre-war cars

FROM PRE-HISTORY TO THE NUCLEAR AGE

It was around ten years ago that Formula 1 teams began to turn to the aeronautical industry rather than the automobile industry for the recruitment of staff and to explore new materials such as carbon, "Kevlar" and high performance metals and alloys, which are now commonplace.

THE 1960s
Drivers started wearing helmets and fireproof overalls and adopted a more reclined position. Engines moved to the rear and the monocoque chassis was introduced. F1 had entered the modern era. For safety reasons, minimum weight was raised first to 450 kg, then to 500 kg

A MAXIMUM OF 12 CYLINDERS
Engine capacity is restricted to 3,500cc and the number of cylinders must not exceed twelve. Turbocharging is not permitted and only reciprocating piston-engines are allowed, a clause that effectively outlaws rotary technology

REAR WINGS
Rear overhang must not be over 50 cm. Wing width is limited to 100 cm whilst their height may not exceed 95 cm

Canon

GEARBOX
A minimum of 4 forward speeds and a maximum of 7. Reverse gear mandatory

THE 1970s
As front radiators moved to the sides, Formula 1 cars took on a more wedge-like shape. Wings, which had already begun to appear towards the end of the 60s, were inverted airplane wings fitted to improve the car's downforce

SEAT AND FULL-HARNESS BELTS
Six-point harness belts are mandatory and must be approved by the FIA

INCONSPICUOUS SUSPENSION
Chrome-plating of suspension wishbones and pull-rods is not permitted

THE 1980s
Ground effect was restricted whilst skirts, aimed at creating a low-pressure zone under the cars, were outlawed in the early 80s. To increase the speed of their cars, teams turned to other means, notably turbo engines capable of power outputs of up to 1,200 bhp

A normally-aspirated Formula 1 car: 750 bhp, 505 kg.

THE 1990s
To halt escalating power outputs, the normally-aspirated 3.5-litre engine was established as the norm for the sport. More recently, electronic driver aids such as ABS, active suspension and traction control have been dropped

COMPARED WITH THE USA

F1 and Indy are the world's two fastest forms of single-seater motor racing. Because of the speeds reached on America's oval circuits, Indy cars are heavier and feature a profiled undertray to keep them 'glued' to the track. F1 cars tend to be more agile and sophisticated than Indy cars, as well as quicker around traditional circuits. But it would be unreasonable to let an F1 car race on oval tracks.

A turbocharged Formula Indy car: 800 bhp, 750 kg.

Formula 1 teams

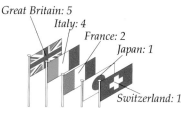

IN THE HISTORY OF F1, not a season passes without the departure of at least one team. Invariably their place is snapped up immediately. Since 1950, no less than 94 teams have tried their hand in F1. Thirteen were present in the 1993 championship, which means that 81 have disappeared over the years. In Formula 1, simply surviving is a victory in itself. The Brabham team, World Champion in 1983, disappeared less than ten years after winning its last world title. Meanwhile, Frank Williams has still not forgotten the somber days of the seventies when he was forced to sell all his personal effects to pay his staff. It is said that the money of sponsors tends to go to the best-equipped teams, and the increase in the budget required to start a team has, over the past decade or so, resulted in a marked rise in professionalism. Since 1988, just four teams have tasted Grand Prix success: Williams, McLaren, Ferrari and Benetton. It is therefore increasingly difficult for a newcomer to make it to the very top.

F1 TEAM NATIONALITIES

Great Britain: 30 (33%)
Italy: 21 (22%)
Germany: 11 (12%)
France: 9 (10%)
USA: 6 (6%)
Australia: 3 (3%)
Rest of the world: 7 (8%)
Japan: 3 (3%)
Switzerland: 3 (3%)

1950-1993

Great Britain: 5
Italy: 4
France: 2
Japan: 1
Switzerland: 1

1993

BRITISH OR ITALIAN
More than half the teams to have taken part in the championship since its creation in 1950 – and nearly three-quarters of those racing in 1993 – were either British or Italian. These nationalities have tended to dominate Formula 1. No other has won a Grand Prix since 1983 (Renault) and none has taken a driver to the Drivers' crown since 1955 (Mercedes).

FORMULA 1 DEBUT

Ferrari: 1950
Lotus: 1958
McLaren: 1966
Ligier: 1976
Minardi: 1985
Larrousse: 1987
Sauber: 1993
1950
1960
Tyrrell: 1970
1970
Williams: 1977
1980
BMS: 1988
1990
Benetton: 1986
Footwork: 1991
Jordan: 1991

REJUVENATION
The arrival of new teams is an ongoing process in Formula 1. More than half the teams on the grid in 1993 had been operating for less than ten years. Benetton, created in 1986 from the former Toleman team, is the 'youngest' to have tasted Grand Prix success.

COATS OF ARMS
All F1 teams have their own logos. Some, however, are more famous than others: Ferrari's prancing horse used to be the personal arms of an Italian pilot shot down during the Great War. For Enzo Ferrari, a friend of the man's parents, it was a way of paying tribute to him. The four interlaced letters on the nose-cone of all Lotus cars are the initials of Anthony Colin Bruce Chapman, the founder of Lotus, who died in 1982.

THIRTEEN TEAMS
A sign of the times and a consequence of the current economic climate is the fact that the number of teams in F1 has fallen consistently since 1989. That year, twenty teams took part in the World Championship, a record in the history of the sport. In 1993, this figure dropped to thirteen.

FOOTWORK
42 Grand Prix

JORDAN
48 Grand Prix

BMS SCUDERIA ITALIA
92 Grand Prix

MINARDI
139 Grand Prix

TYRRELL
336 Grand Prix, 23 wins, 2 titles

LARROUSSE
110 Grand Prix

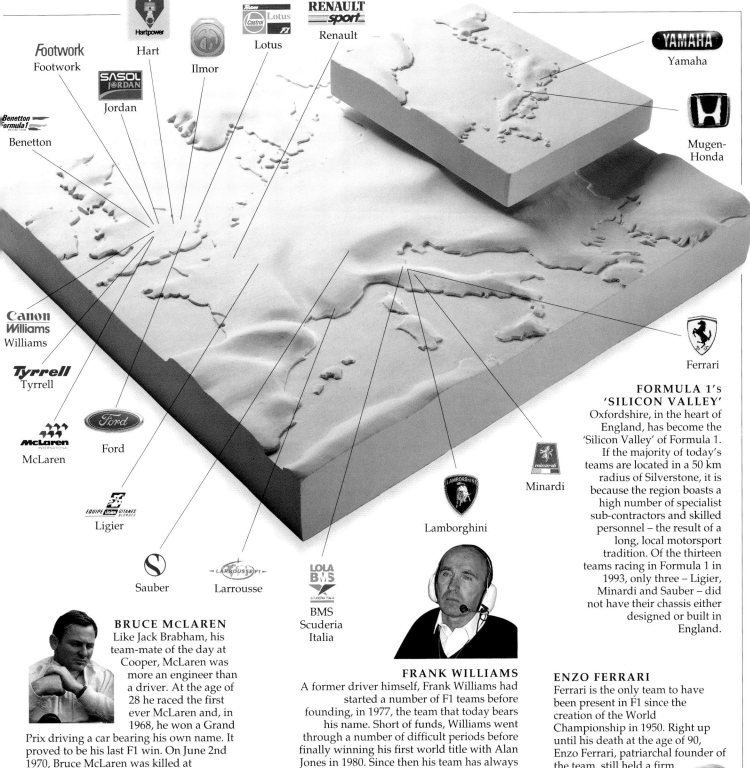

Footwork

Hart

Ilmor

Lotus

Renault

Yamaha

Jordan

Benetton

Mugen-Honda

Canon Williams
Williams

Tyrrell

Ferrari

McLaren

Ford

FORMULA 1's 'SILICON VALLEY'
Oxfordshire, in the heart of England, has become the 'Silicon Valley' of Formula 1. If the majority of today's teams are located in a 50 km radius of Silverstone, it is because the region boasts a high number of specialist sub-contractors and skilled personnel – the result of a long, local motorsport tradition. Of the thirteen teams racing in Formula 1 in 1993, only three – Ligier, Minardi and Sauber – did not have their chassis either designed or built in England.

Ligier

Minardi

Sauber

Larrousse

Lamborghini

BMS Scuderia Italia

BRUCE MCLAREN
Like Jack Brabham, his team-mate of the day at Cooper, McLaren was more an engineer than a driver. At the age of 28 he raced the first ever McLaren and, in 1968, he won a Grand Prix driving a car bearing his own name. It proved to be his last F1 win. On June 2nd 1970, Bruce McLaren was killed at Goodwood. A quarter of a century on, McLaren cars continue to enjoy success.

FRANK WILLIAMS
A former driver himself, Frank Williams had started a number of F1 teams before founding, in 1977, the team that today bears his name. Short of funds, Williams went through a number of difficult periods before finally winning his first world title with Alan Jones in 1980. Since then his team has always figured at the forefront of the sport and, since 1984, only Williams and McLaren have taken a driver to a world title.

ENZO FERRARI
Ferrari is the only team to have been present in F1 since the creation of the World Championship in 1950. Right up until his death at the age of 90, Enzo Ferrari, patriarchal founder of the team, still held a firm rein on the 'Scuderia'. He had created a team in his own image, enchanting yet complicated. Today, it is Fiat who pull the strings. But deep down, Ferrari hasn't changed.

SAUBER
16 Grand Prix

BENETTON
128 Grand Prix, 7 wins

MCLAREN
394 Grand Prix, 104 wins, 9 titles

LOTUS
474 Grand Prix, 79 wins, 6 titles

LIGIER
277 Grand Prix, 8 wins

FERRARI
521 Grand Prix, 103 wins, 9 titles

WILLIAMS
313 Grand Prix, 71 wins, 5 titles

Formula 1 engines

Every year since 1950, a world title has been awarded to the best driver and since 1958 another has been awarded to the best team. Officially, no championship exists for engines. However, in the public's mind, it was clearly Williams and Renault who took the world crown in 1992 and 1993, just as McLaren and Honda had done before them. This is only justice, for in today's Formula 1, the role of the engine is equal to that played by the chassis. Honda eloquently illustrated this by becoming World Champions with Williams in 1987, and then with McLaren in 1988, having switched teams during the winter break.

154 VICTORIES!
The Ford Cosworth DFV V8 is the most successful engine in F1's history. Between 1967 and 1982, it powered practically every car on the grid, to take 154 Grand Prix wins and 10 World Championship titles.

The pneumatic timing system of the Renault V10 has four valves per cylinder

The carbon air-box that feeds the engine's air-injection system is located above the driver's head

The combustion chambers of Renault's V10 engine undergo wind-tunnel testing in order to identify the optimum design for efficient flow

The fuel injection of the Renault V10 is a tube hewn out of solid metal

Titanium bolts are used to mount the gearbox to the engine

Camshafts are now gear-driven. Those of the 1989 RS1 Renault V10 were belt-driven

Pneumatic timing has removed the need for valve springs. Valves are now driven by compressed air

Dry-sump lubrication involves pumping oil into the sump under pressure. Scavenger pumps then pick up the oil and dispatch it to a tank located inside the gearbox housing

In order to do away with flexible pipes, the walls of the cylinder block are cast with internal channels for the circulation of oil and water

RENAULT: THE V10 OPTION
Which is the best solution for F1? V8, V10 or V12? The ideal number of cylinders is a long-standing debate. Based on the same regulations, Ford has elected for a V8, Renault a V10 and Ferrari a V12. Since 1989, when Formula 1 reverted to normally-aspirated engines, the V10 blocks of Honda, then Renault, have won four titles from five.

WHAT GOES INTO AN ENGINE?

Aluminium is the most commonly used metal in today's F1 engines. Cast iron disappeared completely in the 1980s in favour of aluminium, which is lighter. Aluminium has also replaced magnesium, which corrodes in contact with water. Steel has yet to be challenged, however, for moving parts like crankshafts and camshafts, which must withstand the greatest forces.

ALUMINIUM AND STEEL

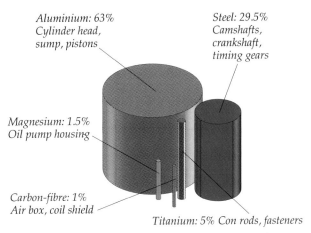

Aluminium: 63%
Cylinder head, sump, pistons

Steel: 29.5%
Camshafts, crankshaft, timing gears

Magnesium: 1.5%
Oil pump housing

Carbon-fibre: 1%
Air box, coil shield

Titanium: 5% Con rods, fasteners

Except for certain parts that need to be made from special materials, Formula 1 engines are principally made from aluminium and steel

EIGHT ENGINES

Eight different engine suppliers were involved in F1 in 1993: Ford, Renault, Ferrari, Yamaha, Mugen-Honda, Ilmor, Lamborghini and Hart. Whilst some of these manufacturers supplied just one team, others supplied a number of outfits, although on differing bases: Williams and Renault, like Benetton and Ford, were partners, whereas McLaren, Minardi, Lotus (all Ford) and Ligier (Renault) paid for their engines.

FORD V8
Benetton, McLaren, Lotus and Minardi

RENAULT V10
Williams and Ligier

MUGEN-HONDA V10
Footwork

YAMAHA V10
Tyrrell

HART V10
Jordan

FERRARI V12
Ferrari, Scuderia Italia

LAMBORGHINI V12
Larrousse

ILMOR V10
Sauber

RENAULT-SPORT: A STAFF OF 150 FOR AN ENGINE

A STAFF OF 150 TO BUILD AN ENGINE

Renault-Sport employs a total staff of around 150: 25 engineers, 20 draughtsmen, 35 engine mechanics, 8 electronics specialists, 20 machinists and fitters, 4 systems engineers, 6 people in charge of test-bench maintenance, 15 in purchasing, production and inspection, and 15 administrative staff.

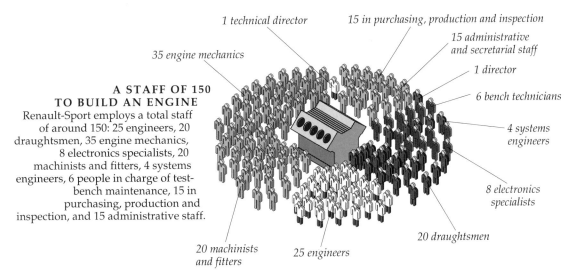

1 technical director
15 in purchasing, production and inspection
35 engine mechanics
15 administrative and secretarial staff
1 director
6 bench technicians
4 systems engineers
8 electronics specialists
20 draughtsmen
20 machinists and fitters
25 engineers

EVOLUTION OF F1 ENGINES

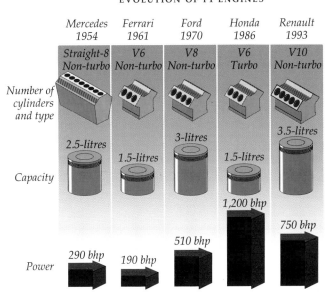

	Mercedes 1954	Ferrari 1961	Ford 1970	Honda 1986	Renault 1993
Number of cylinders and type	Straight-8 Non-turbo	V6 Non-turbo	V8 Non-turbo	V6 Turbo	V10 Non-turbo
Capacity	2.5-litres	1.5-litres	3-litres	1.5-litres	3.5-litres
Power	290 bhp	190 bhp	510 bhp	1,200 bhp	750 bhp

RENAULT V6 TURBO

This engine changed the face of F1. In 1977, nobody believed that a 1.5-litre turbo-charged engine could possibly beat a 3-litre normally-aspirated unit. Renault proved it was possible during what became known as the 'turbo years'. Possibly F1's finest.

TURBO BOOST

Over the years, F1 engines have become more compact, lighter and more fuel-efficient. At the same time, power outputs have risen, reaching a peak during the turbo years (1977-1988). The leading engines of the day – including BMW, Porsche, Renault, Ferrari and Honda – put out more than 1,200 bhp in qualifying specification.

13

Formula 1 engineers

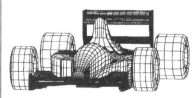

THERE EXIST TWO DISTINCT TYPES of F1 engineers – those who design engines and those who design the chassis. Engine specialists need the technical and financial backing of a major manufacturer and tend to be loyal – either by nature or through necessity – to one firm. Chassis engineers move around more. Whereas before they worked in the shadow of team owners, they have today become aware of their own importance and aware that their expertise is transferable from one team to another. As a result, they have acquired star status in F1, earning salaries of hundreds of thousands of pounds. As with drivers, there exists a transfer market for engineers. An exception is Williams where, in 1977, Frank Williams soon recognised Patrick Head's rare talent and offered him shares in the team.

TECHNICAL DIRECTOR
This is the highest position an engineer can reach in a team. He is the man who oversees everything. An all-rounder, it is he who establishes the overall programme to be followed by the specialist engineers working under him.

JOHN BARNARD
Ferrari
47, British. F1 debut with McLaren in 1981. Returned to Ferrari after a spell with Benetton

2) COMPUTER
Component parts of the car are translated into CAD-CAM language.

1) SKETCHES
The design of a Formula 1 car starts with sketched ideas on a sheet of paper.

INNOVATIONS THAT HAVE CHANGED FORMULA 1
From time to time, engineers' ideas have provided a fresh impulse to F1 design. A few examples:

REAR-MOUNTED ENGINES
Cooper 45, 1958
It was John Cooper who brought a halt to the era of front-mounted engines with the Cooper 45, which took the crown in 1959 and 1960

WINGS
Brabham BT 26, 1968
Jack Brabham was the first to use moveable wings in Formula 1. Outlawed in 1969, they were replaced by fixed wings

IN-BOARD SUSPENSION
Lotus 72, 1970
Having designed the first monocoque chassis in 1962, Colin Chapman introduced in-board suspension and side-mounted radiators in 1970

ROSS BRAWN
Benetton
39, British. F1 debut with Williams in 1976. Has worked with Lola, Arrows and Jaguar. Joined Benetton in 1991

PATRICK HEAD
Williams
47, British. The most loyal of them all. F1 debut with Wolf-Williams in 1976. Has never left Williams since and became a partner in the team in 1977

ADRIAN NEWEY
Williams
35, British. F1 debut with Fittipaldi in 1980. Worked in Indy before returning to F1 with March in 1987. Has been Patrick Head's number 2 at Williams since 1990

NEIL OATLEY
McLaren
42, British. F1 debut with Williams in 1977. Joined Lola in 1984. Two years later, moved to McLaren where he was appointed Chief Designer in 1989

TECHNICAL STAFF AT WILLIAMS
From Technical Director, to Chief Designer and specialist engineers, each is responsible for his own particular field

Managing Director

Technical Director

Manufacturing

Chief Designer

Administration Director

General Management

Race and test teams

Facilities

Team coordination

Systems

Logistics

Programmes

Personnel

Team Manager

Design engineers, research and development engineers

Personnel

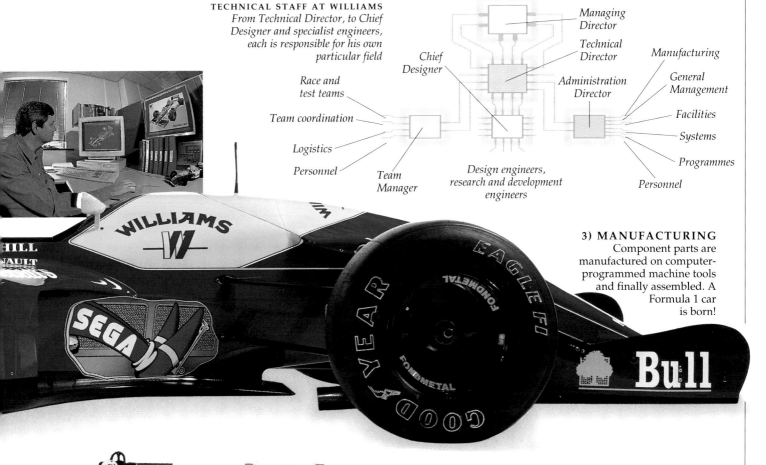

3) MANUFACTURING
Component parts are manufactured on computer-programmed machine tools and finally assembled. A Formula 1 car is born!

GROUND EFFECT
Lotus 78, 1977
Another of Chapman's ideas. The undertray of the Lotus 78 formed an upturned wing, forcing the chassis to the ground. Ground effect had arrived

CARBON BODY
McLaren MP4/1, 1982
Taking over at McLaren, Ron Dennis put his full trust in John Barnard who produced Formula 1's first carbon body

DATA LOGGING
Renault RE60, 1985
An on-board electronic pack recorded revs, pressures and temperatures. More recently, telemetry allowed this data to be transmitted in real time to the pits

RAISED NOSES
March 881, 1988
Raised noses, first seen in 1988, were the idea of Adrian Newey to improve air flow past the chassis

Fuel and tyres

FORMULA 1 CARS USE neither the same tyres nor the same fuels as road cars. The special compounds used in competition tyres provide exceptionally high grip – especially in the wet – whilst fuels are tailor-made especially for F1. Performance, however, does not come cheap. A litre of fuel costs several pounds and a racing tyre will set you back around £700. The sport's leading suppliers leave no stone unturned in their quest to discover the best molecule or the most explosive cocktail.

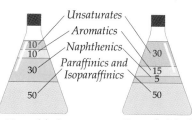

Normal fuel   Formula 1 fuel

ALCHEMY AND PERFORMANCE
The same ingredients go into the fuels that power Formula 1 cars and those available at your local service station. Only the proportions differ.

SPECIAL COMPOUNDS
Tyre technology has made enormous progress since the early part of the century, when motorists ran on rubberised canvas strips. These extremely rigid tyres had a habit of breaking up. Today, the exact formulae used in tyre manufacture are closely-guarded secrets, but principal ingredients include rubber, carbon black, oils, sulphur and additives.

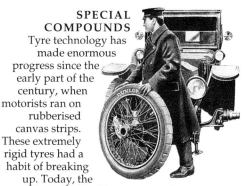

1915

1960

TYRE WARMERS
Formula 1 tyres offer optimum grip at temperatures of around 100°C. This is why special warmers are used to pre-heat the tyres just before they are fitted to the cars. Even so, a full lap must be completed before a tyre reaches peak performance. A technician checks the temperature of the tyres at each pit stop.

FROM ROAD TYRES TO SPECIALIZED RACING RUBBER
The development of special tyres for racing purposes is a fairly recent phenomenon. The first trials took place at the American circuit of Daytona in 1957 and their use became general practice in 1962.

ELF ON POLE POSITION

Elf – the fuel of World Champions. After being dominated by Elf for three seasons, the French oil company's rivals were unable to make up ground in 1993. Research chemists at Elf's Solaize laboratories near Lyon blend special fuels not only for each type of engine, but also for each type of circuit. This work has directly benefitted ordinary commercial fuels. In fact, in line with F1 regulations, Grand Prix fuels are very close to those retailed in service-stations.

FIERCE COMPETITION

For fuel companies, F1 is a highly efficient means of promoting their image. In 1993, no less than six companies – Elf, Agip, Shell, BP, Sasol and Burmah – supplied the F1 grid, and rivalry between them is as fierce as that between the different engine suppliers and chassis builders. In the case of fuel, the battle is won or lost in the laboratory.

Wet-weather tyre

Dry-weather slick

WET AND DRY

The ingredients that go into the manufacture of a Formula 1 tyre have only one purpose – to provide maximum grip in all possible conditions. In 1993, Goodyear's slick tyres came in four different compounds ranging from 'A' (hard) to 'D' (very soft). In wet weather, a fifth option is available featuring a very soft compound and a tread pattern capable of clearing 26 litres of water every second at speeds of up to 300 kph. F1 tyres are tubeless and pressures used vary from 1 to 1.4 bars.

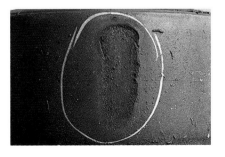

FLAT SPOT

Locked wheels under braking can cause irreparable damage to tyres. The soft compound rubber instantly over-heats and sticks to the track, causing what is known as a flat spot on the tyre's surface.

Formula 1 comparisons

*Price in France in 1993: 55,000 Francs
Length: 343 cm, width: 163 cm*

*Price in France in 1993: 418,000 Francs
Length: 441 cm, width: 165 cm*

*Price in 1993: approx. 4,000,000 Francs
Length: 420 cm, width: 200 cm*

WHAT DO A RENAULT TWINGO, an Alpine A 610 Turbo and a Williams F1 racing car have in common? Answer: four wheels, a steering wheel and a Renault engine. And that's about all. A Formula 1 car is designed to go as fast as possible over a very short distance. The distance of a Grand Prix is 300 km. Should a Formula 1 car break during the 301st kilometre, having passed the chequered flag, then it has done its job. On the other hand, a Twingo or an Alpine A 610 must be capable of exceeding 100,000 kilometres without difficulty.

TWINGO In the hands of Damon Hill, the Twingo took Club Corner at Silverstone at a speed of 80 kph

ALPINE A 610 TURBO
Same day, same circuit, same corner, same driver. 100 kph for the Alpine A 610 Turbo

SPEED
Wide tyres and wings – which have a braking effect – make F1 cars more agile than quick. The Alpine's top speed is only 75 kph less than the Williams-Renault. At Le Mans, sports-prototype cars have been known to exceed 400 kph.

TOP SPEED

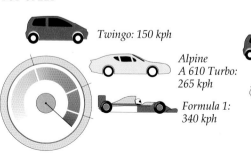

Twingo: 150 kph

Alpine A 610 Turbo: 265 kph

Formula 1: 340 kph

ACCELERATION
If a Twingo, an Alpine and a Formula 1 car set off for a standing start kilometre at the same moment, the F1 car would cover the distance in 12 seconds. In that time, the Alpine would have covered 230 metres and the Twingo just 105 metres. The Alpine would pass the line in 25s, the Twingo in 36s.

Start	250m	500m	750m	1,000m

Twingo: 105m in 12s

Alpine A 610 Turbo: 230m in 12s

Williams-Renault: 1,000m in 12s

BRAKING
Thanks to its light weight, carbon discs and broad tyres, a Formula 1 car is unbeatable when it comes to braking, requiring just 18 metres to brake from 100 kph to standstill.

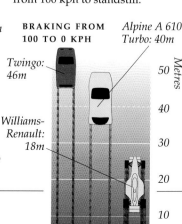

BRAKING FROM 100 TO 0 KPH

Alpine A 610 Turbo: 40m

Twingo: 46m

Williams-Renault: 18m

Metres

50

40

30

20

10

F1 rear tyre
Width: 38 cm
Height: 66 cm

Front tyre
Width: 29 cm
Height: 64 cm

F1 engine:
8, 10 or
12 cylinders,
3,500 cc,
approx. 750 bhp

MAXIMUM POWER

Formula 1 engine manufacturers refuse to reveal exact maximum power values for their creations. In certain cases, the figure is around the 800 bhp mark. Whilst outright power does of course influence a Formula 1 car's top speed, other criteria for evaluating an engine's performance do exist, such as its flexibility or the availability of power across the entire rev-band. A peaky engine, or one that is too bulky or heavy, can upset the balance of a chassis. Nonetheless, maximum power is probably the most readily understood benchmark. With a cubic capacity three times that of the Twingo, an F1 engine is fifteen times more powerful.

Alpine rear tyre
Width: 24.5 cm
Height: 63 cm

Front tyre
Width: 20.5 cm
Height: 60 cm

Alpine engine:
6 cylinders,
2,963 cc,
250 bhp

Twingo rear tyre
Width: 14.5 cm
Height: 54 cm

Front tyre
Width: 14.5 cm
Height: 54 cm

Twingo engine:
4 cylinders,
1,239 cc,
55 bhp

WILLIAMS-RENAULT FW15
Still through Club Corner, still the same day, the Williams-Renault driven by Damon Hill was clocked at 160 kph

FUEL CONSUMPTION

A Formula 1 engine is a real guzzler. At top-speed, 100 litres of fuel are needed to cover 100 km, ten times the requirement of the Twingo. During a Grand Prix, a Formula 1 car consumes between 180 and 200 litres in a distance of 300 km.

**FUEL CONSUMPTION FOR
100 KILOMETRES AT TOP SPEED**

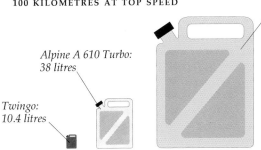

Williams-Renault: 100 litres

Alpine A 610 Turbo: 38 litres

Twingo: 10.4 litres

POWER-TO-WEIGHT RATIO

A Formula 1 car boasts 1 bhp for every 650 grammes of weight. For the Alpine, 1 bhp has to pull 6 kg, and the same figure for the Twingo is 14 kg. Power-to-weight ratio goes a long way towards explaining the staggering performance of Formula 1 cars. They weigh just 505 kg, 5 kg of which are mandatory ballast for cars not carrying on-board TV cameras.

Twingo: 14.4 kg/bhp (790 kg, 55 bhp)

*Alpine A 610 Turbo: 5.7 kg/bhp
(1,420 kg, 250 bhp)*

Williams-Renault: 0.65 kg/bhp (505 kg, 750 bhp)

F1 on the move

As it works its way around the circuits of the world, Formula 1 is like a small town on the move. Each team travels with two, sometimes three transporters, plus one, two, or even three motorhomes that bear the names of sponsors and that serve as base for team personnel and guests. Nothing is spared in the decoration of these gleaming vehicles, and their cost runs into hundreds of thousands of pounds. A Grand Prix paddock is a spectacle in its own right! For Grand Prix outside Europe, equipment is freighted in by specially chartered planes to be stored in crates at the circuits.

THE TRANSPORT BUDGET
To assist teams with the considerable costs involved in transporting personnel and equipment to races (a budget of around £ 2,000,000 for a middle-of-the-grid team), the Formula 1 Constructors' Association (FOCA) takes on board a share of the expenses incurred by the ten best-placed teams in the championship.

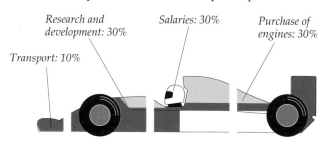

Research and development: 30%   *Salaries: 30%*   *Purchase of engines: 30%*

Transport: 10%

THE RACING TEAM'S BUDGET

UNLOADING
During transport, cars are stowed on upper decks. They are unloaded using an electric tail-lift that also serves as a door when folded in the upright position.

FORMULA 1 HAS PUT ON WEIGHT
Since 1950, the amount of equipment shipped to races for two cars has increased ten-fold. This increase is due to the number of spares carried.

Williams-Renault
25 tonnes

McLaren-Ford
6 tonnes

Ferrari
2.5 tonnes

1950   1970   1993

CUSTOMS CLEARANCE
Formula 1 hates wasting time. Equipment shipped from one circuit to another must be able to pass from country to country with the least fuss possible. It is the team's logistics manager who is responsible for carrying with him the piles of administrative documents required by customs officials, and he never lets them out of his sight.

ENGINES APART

Only one team, Ferrari, produces both its own chassis and engines. All other teams are made up of separate chassis and engine suppliers. In the case of Williams and Ligier, racing cars arrive at the circuit with engines already fitted, whilst spare blocks are shipped independently from Renault's Viry-Châtillon base near Paris. The two meet up at the circuit where Williams and Ligier mechanics are despatched to pick up their precious V10s from the Renault truck. Crates for the attention of the British team are marked with a yellow sticker, those for the French team with a blue sticker.

PELL-MELL

Twenty years ago, tools, spares, cars, and occasionally camp beds for mechanics, were loaded onto trucks pell-mell. Today's semi-trailers are made-to-measure affairs with air-conditioning to ensure pleasant working conditions at all times.

FOUR TIMES AROUND THE WORLD

A Formula 1 team clocks up some 160,000 kilometres every year, the equivalent of four times around the planet. The fifty or so people who make up the race team spend an average of 200 hours each season travelling in planes.

Trucks and trailers are painted in the colours of the team

OPERATING THEATRE

Team transporters are as spotless and tidy as operating theatres. The tools and hardware – screws and fasteners, for example – necessary for the assembly and maintenance of the cars are stored beneath benches along the sides of the trailer. Once the cars themselves have been unloaded, mechanics and engineers have a fully-fitted workshop at their disposal.

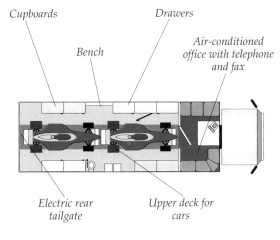

Cupboards

Bench

Drawers

Air-conditioned office with telephone and fax

Electric rear tailgate

Upper deck for cars

TAKING STOCK

As well as cars and engines, leading teams such as Williams-Renault will ship practically their entire workshop to each Grand Prix circuit. Semi-trailers are filled to the brim with sufficient parts to build a complete car many times over. These include:

- body-parts: front and rear wings, undertrays, nose-cones, repair-kits (resin)
- telemetry: aerials, computers, calculators, colour screens, printers
- electrical equipment: generators, voltage regulators
- compressors and oxygen bottles for air tools
- a few hundred kilos of miscellaneous tools
- and even spares to repair... the crates that contain all this!

Formula 1 circuits

IN 43 YEARS, F1 has visited 54 circuits in 24 countries. Since 1984, the number of Grand Prix organised in a single season has been limited to sixteen. Individual countries are able to host just one race, although there are exceptions to this rule. The patronage of San Marino, for example, allows Imola to run a second race in Italy, whilst a "European Grand Prix" also gives UK spectators a second race. The introduction by the FIA of a check list of mandatory requirements for circuits coincided with the disappearance from F1 of such legendary venues as Brands Hatch, Nürburgring and Zandvoort.

Permanent medical centre: Must be located in a protected site close to the pits with operating theatre and resuscitation room

Emergency evacuation helicopter: Neither the race nor practice can start without it

Camera

Camera

Marshal's observation post

NUMBER OF GRAND PRIX HOSTED PER CIRCUIT SINCE 1950

50
40
30
20
10

16 19 20 20 24 27 28 30 40 43

Buenos Aires (Arg.)
Zeltweg (A)
Kyalami (South Africa)
Watkins Glen (USA)
Nürburgring (D)
Silverstone (GB)
Spa-Francorchamps (B)
Zandvoort (NL)
Monaco (MC)
Monza (I)

Track: Between 7 and 11 metres wide and between 3.5 and 7 km in length

Rumble strips: Track-side kerbs to prevent drivers cutting corners

Stands: Must be separated from the track by wire fences and a 1.2 metre high rail

First corner: To avoid tangles, the first corner must be a constant- or widening-radius curve. Cars must be able to take it at 125 kph

Monaco, Spa, Silverstone and Monza all hosted races in the first ever F1 World Championship in 1950. Although their layouts have been revised since, these four circuits have held the highest number of races in the sport's history.

1994 PROVISIONAL CALENDAR

South Africa
Kyalami
March 13th 1994
4.261 km

Brazil
Interlagos
March 27th 1994
4.325 km

Europe
Donington
April 10th 1994
4.020 km

Spain
Barcelona
May 29th 1994
4.747 km

San Marino
Imola
May 1st 1994
5.040 km

Monte-Carlo
Monaco
May 15th 1994
3.328 km

Canada
Montreal
June 12th 1994
4.430 km

France
Magny-Cours
July 3rd 1994
4.271 km

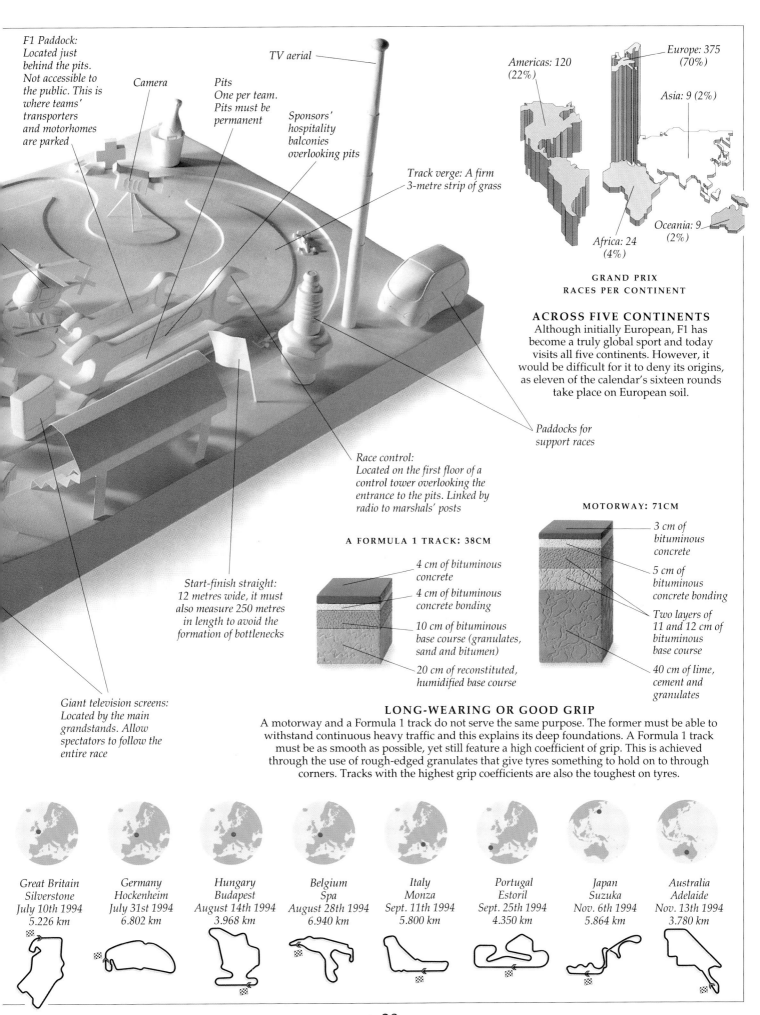

F1 Paddock: Located just behind the pits. Not accessible to the public. This is where teams' transporters and motorhomes are parked

Camera

Pits One per team. Pits must be permanent

TV aerial

Sponsors' hospitality balconies overlooking pits

Track verge: A firm 3-metre strip of grass

Americas: 120 (22%)

Europe: 375 (70%)

Asia: 9 (2%)

Africa: 24 (4%)

Oceania: 9 (2%)

GRAND PRIX RACES PER CONTINENT

ACROSS FIVE CONTINENTS

Although initially European, F1 has become a truly global sport and today visits all five continents. However, it would be difficult for it to deny its origins, as eleven of the calendar's sixteen rounds take place on European soil.

Paddocks for support races

Race control: Located on the first floor of a control tower overlooking the entrance to the pits. Linked by radio to marshals' posts

Start-finish straight: 12 metres wide, it must also measure 250 metres in length to avoid the formation of bottlenecks

Giant television screens: Located by the main grandstands. Allow spectators to follow the entire race

MOTORWAY: 71CM

3 cm of bituminous concrete

5 cm of bituminous concrete bonding

Two layers of 11 and 12 cm of bituminous base course

40 cm of lime, cement and granulates

A FORMULA 1 TRACK: 38CM

4 cm of bituminous concrete

4 cm of bituminous concrete bonding

10 cm of bituminous base course (granulates, sand and bitumen)

20 cm of reconstituted, humidified base course

LONG-WEARING OR GOOD GRIP

A motorway and a Formula 1 track do not serve the same purpose. The former must be able to withstand continuous heavy traffic and this explains its deep foundations. A Formula 1 track must be as smooth as possible, yet still feature a high coefficient of grip. This is achieved through the use of rough-edged granulates that give tyres something to hold on to through corners. Tracks with the highest grip coefficients are also the toughest on tyres.

| Great Britain Silverstone July 10th 1994 5.226 km | Germany Hockenheim July 31st 1994 6.802 km | Hungary Budapest August 14th 1994 3.968 km | Belgium Spa August 28th 1994 6.940 km | Italy Monza Sept. 11th 1994 5.800 km | Portugal Estoril Sept. 25th 1994 4.350 km | Japan Suzuka Nov. 6th 1994 5.864 km | Australia Adelaide Nov. 13th 1994 3.780 km |

Officials

A FORMULA 1 GRAND PRIX COULD NOT BE ORGANISED without the presence of FIA officials. As representatives of motorsport's international governing body, these are the people who ensure that regulations are complied with at all times. Their individual roles are set out in the 'Yellow Book', an indispensable 'bible' comprising nearly 600 pages of regulations covering all aspects of motorsport events organised under the jurisdiction of the Fédération Internationale de l'Automobile. Certain officials work full-time for the FIA and attend all F1 meetings. Others are nominated for individual races by the national governing body of the country hosting the race. The full list of officials necessary for the successful running of an event would be too long to recount, but these pages provide a brief insight into the duties and functions of the principal ones.

Max Mosley
FIA President

THE STARTER
Roland Bruynseraede has been responsible for 'unleashing the pack' at all Grand Prix races since 1987. Roland is also Race Director and Chairman of the FIA's Safety Commission.

RACE DIRECTOR
The Race Director is responsible for the smooth overall running of the meeting. Constantly in contact with all other officials, his duties range from the checking of competition numbers to ensuring that cars are correctly positioned on the grid, chairing a Drivers' Briefing on the morning before the race, and recommending penalties for anyone failing to comply with the regulations. He is the most important single person at a meeting.

MEDICAL OFFICER
A Chief Medical Officer, Dr. Sid Watkins, has been nominated by the FIA to attend all World Championship races, where his role is to supervise all medical matters.

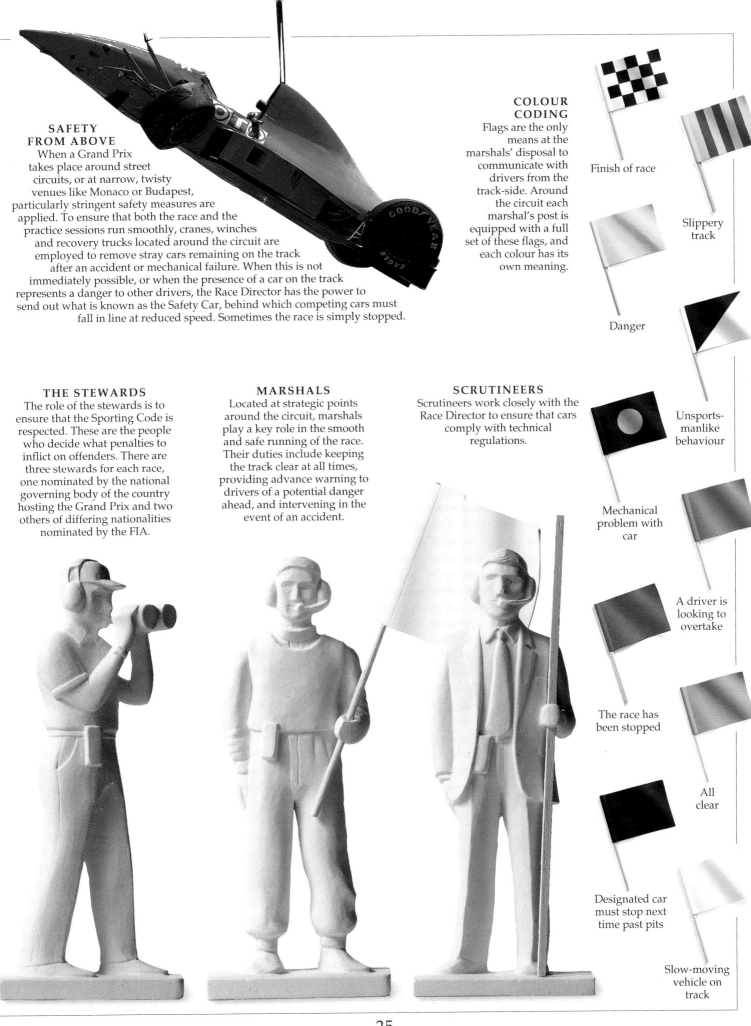

SAFETY FROM ABOVE

When a Grand Prix takes place around street circuits, or at narrow, twisty venues like Monaco or Budapest, particularly stringent safety measures are applied. To ensure that both the race and the practice sessions run smoothly, cranes, winches and recovery trucks located around the circuit are employed to remove stray cars remaining on the track after an accident or mechanical failure. When this is not immediately possible, or when the presence of a car on the track represents a danger to other drivers, the Race Director has the power to send out what is known as the Safety Car, behind which competing cars must fall in line at reduced speed. Sometimes the race is simply stopped.

COLOUR CODING

Flags are the only means at the marshals' disposal to communicate with drivers from the track-side. Around the circuit each marshal's post is equipped with a full set of these flags, and each colour has its own meaning.

Finish of race

Slippery track

Danger

Unsportsmanlike behaviour

Mechanical problem with car

A driver is looking to overtake

The race has been stopped

All clear

Designated car must stop next time past pits

Slow-moving vehicle on track

THE STEWARDS

The role of the stewards is to ensure that the Sporting Code is respected. These are the people who decide what penalties to inflict on offenders. There are three stewards for each race, one nominated by the national governing body of the country hosting the Grand Prix and two others of differing nationalities nominated by the FIA.

MARSHALS

Located at strategic points around the circuit, marshals play a key role in the smooth and safe running of the race. Their duties include keeping the track clear at all times, providing advance warning to drivers of a potential danger ahead, and intervening in the event of an accident.

SCRUTINEERS

Scrutineers work closely with the Race Director to ensure that cars comply with technical regulations.

25

Life in the pits

0600	Wake-up
0700	Set off for the racetrack
0730	Arrive at the racetrack
0735	Preparing the car
0920	Fitting wheels and nose cone
0930	Free practice, adjustments
1100	End of session, checking
1120	Snack
1130	Preparing car for timed laps
1300	Official timed practice
1400	Draining petrol and oil
1500	Lunch
1530	Preparing the car for the race: changing engine, suspension, gearbox, wheel bearings, radiators
2230	Dinner in the motorhome
2400	Return to the hotel

TEAMS WILL BEGIN TO ARRIVE AT A CIRCUIT on the Wednesday preceding the race and leave again on the Sunday evening. Each team works out of pits allocated to teams on the basis of their position in the previous year's World Championship, and this order does not change once the season is under way. For four days the pits are a buzz of activity. Entry is strictly controlled and even the media and photographers do not escape surveillance. Telemetry monitors are hidden away at the back of the pits behind tarpaulin enclosures. Mechanics continue to work on cars during the evening and into the night, well after the last spectator has left the circuit.

A DAY IN THE LIFE
In the course of a Grand Prix, team mechanics will spend a minimum of sixteen hours per day at the circuit. Both lunch and dinner are taken at the team's motorhome. Should a car be damaged during practice, mechanics might even have to work through the night to carry out necessary repairs. They fly home on the Sunday evening in order to be back at work the following morning.

A HIVE OF ACTIVITY
At a Grand Prix, the pits tend to resemble a busy beehive. Some fifty people, from the drivers themselves to the security guard, work in the Williams pits at any one time.

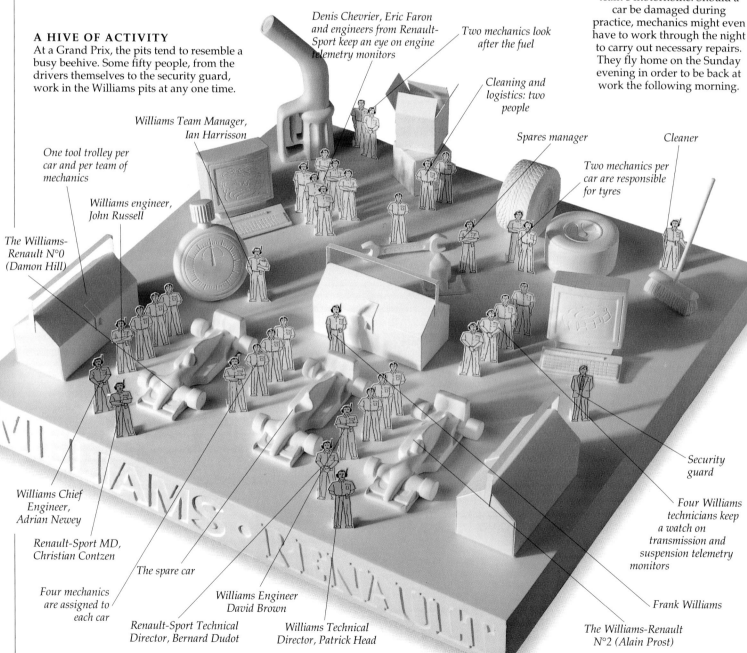

Denis Chevrier, Eric Faron and engineers from Renault-Sport keep an eye on engine telemetry monitors

Two mechanics look after the fuel

Cleaning and logistics: two people

Spares manager

Cleaner

Two mechanics per car are responsible for tyres

Williams Team Manager, Ian Harrisson

One tool trolley per car and per team of mechanics

Williams engineer, John Russell

The Williams-Renault N°0 (Damon Hill)

Williams Chief Engineer, Adrian Newey

Renault-Sport MD, Christian Contzen

The spare car

Four mechanics are assigned to each car

Renault-Sport Technical Director, Bernard Dudot

Williams Engineer David Brown

Williams Technical Director, Patrick Head

Security guard

Four Williams technicians keep a watch on transmission and suspension telemetry monitors

Frank Williams

The Williams-Renault N°2 (Alain Prost)

SWIFT 'N SURE
Formula 1 mechanics are the fastest in the world. The outcome of a race can often depend on the swiftness and reliability of their work.

ENGINE
An emergency engine swap takes one hour...

Radios permit team managers to communicate with drivers and to issue instructions to mechanics once the race is under way

TEAM CLOTHING
Light shirts and shorts in hot weather, trousers for cooler climes. The traditional oily overalls that F1 mechanics used to wear were dropped a long time ago in favour of today's more dashing team clothing, more in keeping with the high-tech image of F1. The return of mid-race refuelling in 1994 means mechanics, like their Indy racing counterparts, will have to wear helmets and flame-resistant overalls during races.

Woollen gloves protect hands against heat during tyre changes

With the return of mid-race refuelling in 1994, mechanics will have to wear flame-resistant overalls

In Formula 1, team colours have even found their way onto footwear

GEARBOX
...whilst a gearbox takes just half an hour to change

BENETTON   FERRARI   FOOTWORK   JORDAN   LARROUSSE   LIGIER   LOTUS

McLAREN   MINARDI   SAUBER   SCUDERIA ITALIA   TYRRELL   WILLIAMS

SHOCK ABSORBERS
Twelve minutes to change all four shock absorbers...

Television coverage of the race   *Lap-by-lap positions and times*   *Engine telemetry data*

PIT CREW CLOTHING
Clothing worn by mechanics and engineers depicts the colours of the team's main sponsors. Teams even supply personnel with official travel-wear – significantly more discreet – for travel by plane from one race to another.

TV MONITORS
To keep a permanent eye on the performance of his car, an engine technician has three screens at his disposal. The first displays a variety of technical data concerning the engine's performance, a television monitor allows him to follow the race itself, whilst a third screen provides lap times and positions.

UMBRELLAS UP
As cars wait on the grid before the start, a team member will hold an umbrella over the driver's head. Not only does this provide protection against rain or intense heat, it also provides an additional opportunity to get sponsors' names in camera shot.

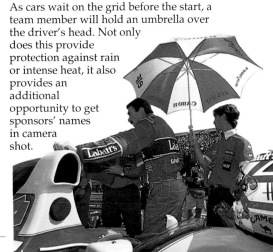

PEDAL BOX
... and just ten minutes to fit pedal box, seat and harness into the spare car

Formula 1 drivers

REACHING THE TOP OF THE FORMULA 1 LADDER takes talent and courage...
and a certain amount of luck. Statistics suggest that your chances of success are better
if you start out young and are a national of a country where motorsports have a deeply-
rooted tradition. Of the 543 drivers from 31 different countries to have raced in Formula 1 since
1950, half of them hailed from Great Britain, France or Italy. Indeed, two-thirds of 1993's line-up
came from these three countries, where racing is
a way of life and where young talent gets a real
opportunity to come to the fore. Like tennis and
football, Formula 1 has not escaped the baby-
champion phenomenon. At the age of just 14,
more than half of today's grid were already out
racing karts. Gone are the days when the likes of
Graham Hill could pass their driving test at the
age of 24 and go on to become World
Champion... twice.

NATIONALITIES OF F1 DRIVERS (1950-1993)

France: 61 (11%)
Great Britain: 131 (25%)
Belgium: 18 (3%)
Germany: 38 (7%)
Switzerland: 21 (4%)
Italy: 74 (14%)
USA: 44 (8%)
Rest of world: 101 (17%)
Brazil: 16 (3%)
Argentina: 20 (4%)
South Africa: 19 (4%)

THE 1993 LINE-UP
Of the drivers racing in F1 in 1993, some, like Capelli
and Barbazza, left the sport in mid-season, their drives
snapped up by the likes of Martini and Boutsen. The
Belgian in turn called it a day after Spa whilst in Estoril
Alain Prost announced his decision to retire from F1.

WHERE DO THEY COME FROM?
Since the creation of Formula 1, one driver in four has been
British, one in two has hailed from Great Britain, France or Italy,
whilst two out of three were European-born. At the other end of
the scale, five countries have produced just one Formula 1
driver: Venezuela, Columbia, Monaco, Thailand and Chile.

| MICHELE ALBORETO 37, Italy | JEAN ALESI 29, France | PHILIPPE ALLIOT 39, France | MICHAEL ANDRETTI 31, USA | LUCA BADOER 22, Italy | FABRIZIO BARBAZZA 30, Italy | RUBENS BARRICHELLO 21, Brazil |

| MIKA HAKKINEN 25, Finland | JOHNNY HERBERT 32, GB | DAMON HILL 31, GB | UKYO KATAYAMA 30, Japan | J.J. LEHTO 27, Finland | PIERLUIGI MARTINI 32, Italy | RICCARDO PATRESE 39, Italy |

KART KIDS

Twenty of the thirty-one drivers in F1 in 1993 used to race karts when they were younger. Indeed, the likes of Prost, Senna, Schumacher, Alesi and Patrese are all past World Champions of the sport. Initially considered racing's poorer cousin and a sport that encouraged bad reflexes, karting eventually came of age in the 1970s when it produced champions of the calibre of Emerson Fittipaldi and Ronnie Peterson. They were eloquent proof that a successful background in karts could genuinely help launch a career in F1. Others soon followed their example and there are few young drivers today who didn't race karts before moving on to a scholarship or a one-make formula.

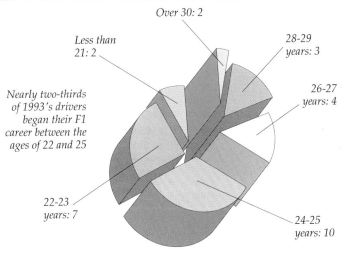

Over 30: 2

Less than 21: 2

28-29 years: 3

Nearly two-thirds of 1993's drivers began their F1 career between the ages of 22 and 25

26-27 years: 4

22-23 years: 7

24-25 years: 10

AGES OF 1993'S DRIVERS
AT THE TIME OF THEIR FORMULA 1 DEBUT

DRIVING SCHOLARSHIPS

Competition driving schools exist in many countries, but the French system has proved a particularly successful model – the prize for scholarship winners is a full season in Formula Renault. Of the eighteen French drivers to have reached F1 in the past decade, ten were former scholarship winners, including Prost, Pironi, Tambay and Arnoux. Not winning the scholarship does not necessarily spell the end of a racing career. Alliot and Laffite were beaten in their respective finals, whilst Alesi and Gachot were both dominated by Eric Bernard during one hotly-disputed year.

SINGLE-MAKE FORMULAE

Formula Renault and Formula Ford exist in many European countries, whilst Formula Fiat enjoys popular success in Italy. The leading manufacturers involved in motorsport have long organised such promotional formulae aimed at giving young drivers a chance to cut their teeth at low cost. Prost won the French Formula Renault Championship when he was just 21, and Senna left his mark on the British Formula Ford Championship.

| GERHARD BERGER 34, Austria | MARK BLUNDELL 27, GB | THIERRY BOUTSEN 36, Belgium | MARTIN BRUNDLE 34, GB | IVAN CAPELLI 30, Italy | ANDREA DE CESARIS 34, Italy | ERIK COMAS 30, France | CHRISTIAN FITTIPALDI 22, Brazil |

| ALAIN PROST 38, France | MICHAEL SCHUMACHER 25, Germany | AYRTON SENNA 33, Brazil | AGURI SUZUKI 33, Japan | DEREK WARWICK 39, GB | KARL WENDLINGER 25, Austria | ALESSANDRO ZANARDI 27, Italy |

Driver racewear

BACK IN 1950, THE LIKES OF FANGIO AND ASCARI used to race in shirt-sleeves and trousers. Mike Hawthorn even went so far as to sport a bow tie! When an accident occurred – and alas they were all too frequent – the fate of a driver was often in the lap of the gods. All that is history now. Today's textiles have made staggering progress and modern drivers must wear special clothing bearing the international motorsport governing body's tag of approval. Indeed, the FIA's standards are extremely high in this domain, especially concerning flame resistance. A fully-kitted driver must be able to escape unscathed if caught for up to twelve seconds in a 700°C hydrocarbon blaze.

THE HELMET
Each driver gets through between three and five helmets in the course of a season. Besides providing effective head protection, they also sport the driver's personal colours and those of his sponsors.

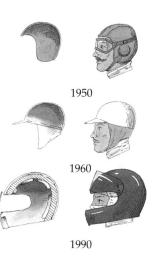

1950

1960

1990

FORMULA 1 TECHNOLOGY
Today's full-face helmets are manufactured from the same materials used in the manufacture of a Formula 1 car. They are even subjected to wind-tunnel tests.

EARPLUGS
Special earplugs protect drivers' eardrums. In certain cases, they house radio ear-pieces.

NECK STRAP AND COLLAR
This limits head movement and prevents neck muscle fatigue at circuits with long, fast corners.

BALACLAVA
The fire-resistant cloth provides added protection against fire.

FROM LEATHER TO NOMEX
In 1950, drivers wore simple leather head-gear which afforded excellent protection only against the wind. This was later replaced by helmets made first from papier-maché, then fiberglass. A modern full-face helmet weighs just 1.2 kg, half the weight of the first models that appeared back in 1968. The Lexan visor, which has replaced the glass goggles of yesteryear, will protect against a stone catapulted at 500 kph.

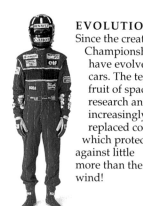

EVOLUTION
Since the creation of the World Championship, driver overalls have evolved as much as the cars. The textiles used are the fruit of space research and have increasingly replaced cotton, which protected against little more than the wind!

PROTECTION
Thanks to impact-absorbing helmets and flame-resistant overalls, drivers are no longer without protection in the case of an accident.

| Michele Alboreto | Jean Alesi | Philippe Alliot | Michael Andretti | Luca Badoer | Fabrizio Barbazza | Rubens Barrichello | Gerhard Berger | Mark Blundell | Thierry Boutsen | Martin Brundle | Ivan Capelli | Erik Comas |

HOT UNDIES

Driver underwear isn't in the least suggestive and, even in the case of lady drivers, lace frills are out of the question. Because of its flame-resistant qualities, "Nomex" is the only authorised material. Socks, T-shirt and long-johns are mandatory underneath overalls.

A STEADY HAND

"Nomex" gloves provide the best protection against fire. Palms are trimmed in leather to ensure optimum grip on the suede steering wheel. Gloves are worn very tight and held in place with a "Velcro" strap.

"NOMEX" ARMOUR

A driver's overalls are his main line of defence against burns. Tailored from flame-resistant "Nomex" cloth, they guarantee protection for twelve seconds in a hydrocarbon blaze at 700°C. All threads, and even advertising patches, must meet the same standards.

FOOT SURE

Race shoes are made from leather and are padded with foam to protect against knocks in the cockpit. For maximum fire resistance, they are finished in "Nomex" and soles are made from high-grip rubber.

Andrea de Cesaris | Christian Fittipaldi | Johnny Herbert | Damon Hill | Ukyo Katayama | J. J. Lehto | Riccardo Patrese | Alain Prost | Michael Schumacher | Ayrton Senna | Aguri Suzuki | Derek Warwick | Karl Wendlinger | Alessandro Zanardi

Athletes in their own right

FORMULA 1 DRIVERS CAN BE LIKENED TO BOTH SPRINTERS and long-distance runners. Make no mistake, keeping a Formula 1 car on the track at speeds of up to 300 kph is a physically exhausting business requiring considerable stamina. The likes of Prost, Senna, Hill and Schumacher are all genuine athletes in their own right and owe their shape to the preparation they put in away from the circuits. Training for this level of motorsport includes developing the reflexes needed to keep control of a car putting out something like 750 bhp. Muscle-building – especially of the arms, back, neck and stomach – helps cope with centrifugal force, which can literally take your breath away and can put the neck under tremendous strain through fast corners. Like a long-distance runner, a Formula 1 driver must also accustom his body, and particularly the heart, to sustained effort over a long period. Last but not least, he must lead a perfectly healthy lifestyle, control his feelings and develop his concentration.

A STRONG ARM
It takes strong arms to drive a Formula 1 car. It is therefore important to build up the muscles of the upper limbs and shoulders in order to go the distance without running the risk of getting cramp.

SUSTAINING THE EFFORT
To evaluate a driver's physical fitness, one of the more commonly used tests involves measuring the maximum amount of oxygen used whilst cycling on an exercise bike. A fit athlete uses oxygen more efficiently than a sedentary person, a faculty which makes him able to respond more easily when sustained effort is required.

AN EXHAUSTING BUSINESS
Even for the fittest of drivers, a Formula 1 Grand Prix is an exhausting exercise. On top of fatigue resulting from intense physical effort, drivers also suffer from the effects of acceleration, vibration and heat. Cockpits are generally 10°C hotter than the outside temperature.

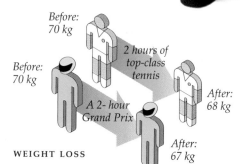

Before: 70 kg

2 hours of top-class tennis

Before: 70 kg

A 2-hour Grand Prix

After: 68 kg

After: 67 kg

WEIGHT LOSS

32

TAKING THE STRAIN

The above machine measures the strength of neck muscles. The driver pushes with his neck alternately to the left and right as hard as he can whilst the machine records the rate at which fatigue sets in. Neck muscles are subjected to considerable strain under cornering. Centrifugal forces can multiply the weight of the head and helmet by a factor of up to four!

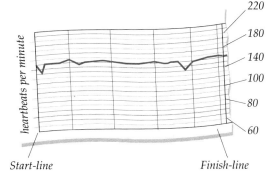

heartbeats per minute

220
180
140
100
80
60

Start-line   *Finish-line*

HEARTBEAT

The above cardiac print-out is that of Philippe Alliot during a lap of Estoril in Portugal. The peaks correspond to zones of braking into corners and the troughs show where the French driver was able to recover along the straights. In a test involving similar levels of effort back at the clinic, Alliot's average heartbeat would probably not exceed 130 beats per minute compared with the 160 recorded on the graph. The difference is due to the stress of driving a Formula 1 car.

STEERING CLEAR OF EXCESS

To ensure the most balanced diet possible, Formula 1 drivers banish all forms of excess. Alcohol and stimulants – coffee, cola-based drinks – are out of the question, and fat intake is kept to an absolute minimum. Main courses generally consist of grilled white meat or fish served with greens, rice or pasta. Indeed, drivers tend to be big consumers of pasta products since they are a valuable source of slow-burning sugars, which means energy is released progressively for greater endurance. As for doping, no case has ever been recorded by the FIA.

THE EFFECTS OF RACING DRIVING ON THE BODY

NECK
A car's tendency to lift over bumps can result in bad muscle strain

COCCYX
The coccyx absorbs shocks caused by uneven track surfaces

THUMBS
Thumbs can be dislocated by the steering wheel if kerbs are taken at speed

KNEES
The top of the fibula is especially prone to knocks in the cockpit

EYES
Certain vibrations can hasten eye fatigue and lead to loss of attention

ELBOWS
Elbows take a lot of bangs against the cockpit

RIBS
Ribs can occasionally fracture as a result of driving over kerbs

FEET
Frequent heavy braking can cause painful soles

CONCENTRATION

Whilst not all drivers have perfect vision, their attention span is longer than average and their resistance to eye fatigue is high.

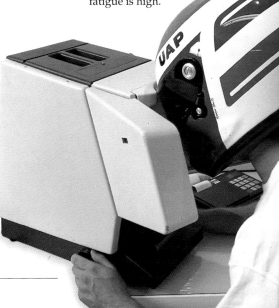

SOME DRIVERS WEAR GLASSES!

Formula 1 drivers are not supermen. Although their level of physical fitness is well above average, some do have eyesight problems. Ivan Capelli, for example, wears glasses under his helmet, as does Erik Comas, although in the Frenchman's case they are sunglasses, which he prefers to using a tinted visor.

The cockpit of a Formula 1 car

DESPITE THE INCREASINGLY WIDESPREAD USE OF TECHNOLOGY and electronics in Formula 1, the driver remains very much sole master on board. He alone can decide whether or not to make use of the aids at his disposal. Should he choose to, it is up to him to adjust settings to the best of his judgement. Suspension stiffness, engine parameters, brake balance and other features are there to enhance performance and not transform the driver into some sort of automatic pilot. Squeezed into his cockpit, the driver must have everything within easy reach or sight, including a whole host of switches and dials that he must be able to use with a minimum of effort. To the man-in-the-street however, there is one glaring absence – there is no speedometer. Instead, it is the rev-counter that informs the driver whether or not the car is going flat out with the engine screaming at full stretch.

1950

1960

1970

1980

FIGHTER PLANE

But for the lack of radar, the cockpit of a Formula 1 car could be mistaken for that of a plane. Centre-piece of the instrument-panel is the liquid-crystal display which, amongst many other functions, can even tell a driver the gap separating him from the car in front or behind. Indeed, thanks to telemetry, anything is possible. As F1 has evolved, cockpits have been increasingly invaded by electronics. The number of buttons, switches and dials has practically tripled over the past decade. The likes of Fangio could be forgiven for feeling lost in a Formula 1 car of the nineties!

FROM NEEDLES TO LIQUID CRYSTALS

Instrument panels in F1 have evolved considerably, with liquid-crystal displays and warning lights replacing the needle-gauge of yesteryear. Today, there are practically no limits to the information a driver can have at his fingertips.

34

TAILOR-MADE DISCOMFORT

Seats are moulded to the exact dimensions of drivers' bodies. Totally devoid of any sort of padding, their sole function is to hold the driver firmly inside the cockpit.

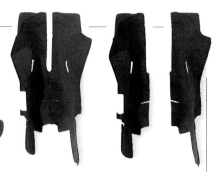

SEAT
Moulded directly around the driver's back, the two carbon shells are assembled together before being trimmed with leather. This helps prevent the body sliding in the seat.

THE INSTRUMENTS OF THE WILLIAMS-RENAULT

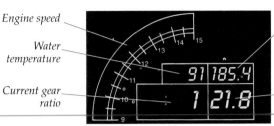

Engine speed

Water temperature

Current gear ratio

Fuel remaining

Lap time

A driver can consult any one of 63 pieces of information concerning the engine

Switch for the red rear warning light, mandatory in case of poor visibility

Rev-limiter override: allows maximum engine speed, pre-programmed by the engine's electronic control unit (ECU), to be overridden

Brake balance. The front-rear split in braking effort is adjustable

Starter switch

Neutral warning light

Battery cut-off switch

Air-fuel mixture adjustment

Activator for fire-fighting system

Active-suspension warning light

Active-suspension roll and stiffness adjustment

Button for saving data onto a floppy disc located in the heart of the car's electronic management system

Radio switch

Traction-control adjustment

Setting up a Formula 1 car

To be 100% competitive, a Formula 1 car must be adjusted – or 'set up' – to suit the characteristics of the circuit on which it is to race. Every time a new track is visited, or each time weather conditions change, settings are revised. Often, previous experience of a circuit or data recorded during previous seasons mean a certain amount of work can be prepared in advance back at base. However, fine-tuning will always be necessary once at the circuit. Setting up a car is a long and difficult job. Literally hundreds of permutations are possible – especially with cars featuring active suspension – and practically all engine and chassis components are adjustable. But whilst searching for the ideal set up can be a complex business, drivers know that the reward for their labour is being able to race a car at the peak of its potential.

REAR WING
Rear downforce can be modified by adjusting the angle and/or dimensions of the rear wing

TOE-IN AND CAMBER
Understeer and oversteer can be compensated for by adjusting the angle of the front and rear wheels

GEARBOX
Gearing should be selected in response to the circuit's characteristics

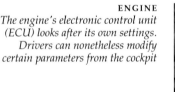

ENGINE
The engine's electronic control unit (ECU) looks after its own settings. Drivers can nonetheless modify certain parameters from the cockpit

BALANCE
Causes of understeer or oversteer can be very simple – a driver turning in too late for a corner, for example, or accelerating too early out of it. Sometimes, however, the reason can be more complicated and can arise from a poor set up. Insufficient downforce at the front or rear, low grip as a result of under-inflated tyres or an incorrectly-adjusted differential can result in mediocre overall balance.

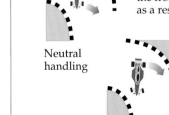

Understeer

Neutral handling

Oversteer

GROUND CLEARANCE
A car's ground clearance can affect its balance (understeer or oversteer) and can be adjusted by modifying the length of the pull-rods or, in the case of an 'active' car, by changing the suspension's electronic programming

EVERYTHING ON A FORMULA 1 CAR IS ADJUSTABLE
From steering wheel to engine, from pedals to the angle of the wheels, from ground clearance to aerodynamics, the majority of parts on a Formula 1 car are adjustable. And those that aren't can be replaced! As a general rule, during a test session, a driver will go out for three laps at a time, stopping at his pits between each series to talk with his engineer. All adjustments are carefully noted and, after the session, findings are compared with telemetry data-printouts.

DIFFERENT SETTINGS FOR RAIN OR SHINE

In wet weather, the critical requirements are brakes and traction and getting power to the ground efficiently. Cars will tend to run with more wing, whilst cooling ducts for brakes and engine will be completely or partially covered to help these organs reach their ideal working temperature more quickly.

DRY WEATHER *Minimum ground clearance (around 10 mm)*	*Low tyre-pressure*	*Reduced wing for low drag*	*Brake cooling ducts fully open to cool discs*	*Hard springs*	*Engine cooling ducts fully open to keep engine at ideal temperature*
WET WEATHER *High ground clearance to deal with increased travel built into rain tyres*	*Higher tyre pressure to 'open up' grooves of tread pattern*	*Increased wing for more downforce*	*Brake cooling ducts covered over to reduce cooling of discs*	*Softer springs*	*Engine cooling ducts partially covered to help the engine reach ideal working temperature*

SIDE PODS
Opening or closing air cooling ducts to engine can help raise or lower engine temperature

FRONT WING
Changing the size of the front wing alters the downforce at the front and consequently modifies the car's overall balance

TYRE PRESSURE
For optimum grip, tyres must be at their ideal working temperature, which is influenced by tyre pressure

BRAKE COOLING DUCTS
The quantity of cooling air reaching brakes influences their temperature and therefore their efficiency. Today's carbon brakes are at their most effective between 350 and 500°C

SUSPENSION
Soft or hard, suspension settings have a significant influence on the car's overall performance (cornering speeds, ground clearance along straights, brake balance and even traction)

STREAMLINED AND ECONOMICAL
The performance of a saloon car such as the Safrane depends on the fluidity of its lines. Effective streamlining helps reduce fuel consumption

HIGH DRAG COEFFICIENT
The 'open-wheel' design and down-forcing wings of a Formula 1 car mean that its drag coefficient is inferior to that of the Safrane

SUCKED TO THE GROUND
The aerodynamic qualities of a Formula 1 car enable it to take corners at high speed as the front and rear wings help keep it 'glued' to the ground. Wings can be adjusted by changing their angle or by adding counter flaps at each end. The suction effect, generated by a combination of downforce and a zone of low pressure created underneath the car as it travels at speeds of up to 300 kph, means it could theoretically be driven across a ceiling.

Driving techniques

A FORMULA 1 CAR IS A BRUTISH MONSTER that needs handling with great caution. Just keeping it in a straight line with something in the order of 750 bhp strapped to your back is a highly delicate exercise. The slightest error and you're into a spin, or even off the track. Drivers who make it into Formula 1 generally have at least ten years' racing experience behind them. Whatever their car, the basic principles of competition driving – position of hands, footwork, braking points, turn-in points, etc – are the same as when they set out in the sport.

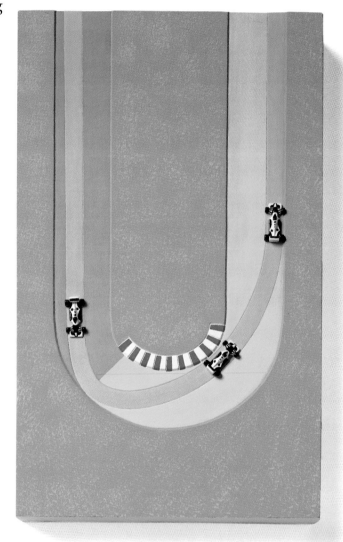

FAST CORNERS
In order to lose a minimum of speed through two consecutive fast corners, drivers look for the straightest line between the two, passing from apex to apex to get in line and re-accelerate as early as possible.

HAIRPINS
Drivers brake in a straight line (red zone) before turning-in late at the outside of the corner. Entry into the corner is 'sacrificed' in order to have as straight a line possible out of it and therefore to be in a position to re-accelerate very early.

S-BENDS
In this case, the first corner is tighter than the second. A driver will brake before the apex of the first (red zone) and, as soon as he turns in, he will aim for the following apex to 'open out' the next corner. He can re-accelerate as soon as he has finished braking for the first corner.

HANDS ON THE WHEEL
Only half a turn is required to go from lock to lock and drivers need never take their hands off the steering wheel. Even for the tightest of hairpins, simply crossing the wrists is sufficient to be at maximum lock.

Along straights, hands should be positioned at 'quarter-to-three'

Through fast corners, the 'inside' hand 'pulls' the wheel

Arms might cross to achieve full lock through a hairpin

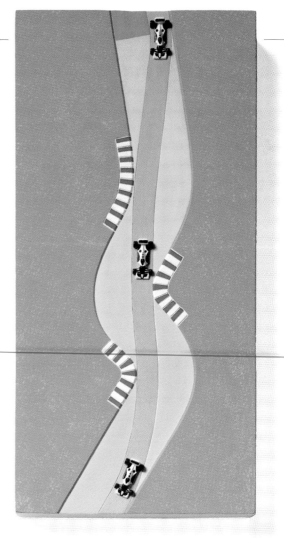

CHICANES

Generally added with a view to slowing speeds along a fast straight, chicanes must be tackled with extreme caution. Number one priority is to maintain as much momentum as possible. Drivers must therefore try to keep the straightest line possible and keep movement of the steering wheel to a minimum.

SPIN

A spin is the result of a sudden loss of grip of the rear wheels due to a poor racing line, excessive speed or because a driver has re-accelerated too hard. A spin can happen as easily at 50 kph as it can at 250 kph.

DOUBLE-DECLUTCHING

Earlier Formula 1 cars had no synchromesh, so drivers had to double-declutch, blipping the throttle with the car in neutral before changing down a gear.

PROST: SMOOTH

Alain Prost's style is very smooth. His lines are straight out of the text book, and a minimum of steering wheel movement makes his driving relatively unspectacular – although highly effective.

SENNA: OVERSTEER

Ayrton Senna drives more on oversteer. He is in a class of his own when the going gets slippery and he basically applies the same techniques he developed in his karting days.

SCHUMACHER: TRUE GRIT

Michael Schumacher doesn't drive – he fights with the track. Extraordinarily aggressive at the wheel, he brakes late and accelerates early. His four-wheel drifts are especially spectacular.

Electronics in Formula 1

IN 1989, FORMULA 1 BECAME aware of what electronics could do for performance. Since then, computers and microchips have become a key feature of car design and an indispensable aid in optimising factors such as cornering speeds, driving comfort and remote management of engine and chassis parameters. Teams' ranks have been swollen with armies of electronics and systems experts who, engineers maintain, could soon enable a car to lap without a driver at the wheel. The FIA has decided to step in however and, as from 1994, the majority of these so-called driver aids have been outlawed.

SEMI-AUTOMATIC GEARBOX
Reduces time required to change gear and allows hands to stay on the wheel at all times. Eliminates the risk of over-revving engines. Operated by two control switches located behind the wheel

ABS
Reduces braking distances to a minimum and eliminates the risk of damaging tyres through the locking of brakes

FORMULA 1 OR VIDEO GAMES?
The high-tech image of F1 has attracted a number of sponsors specialising in leading-edge technology. Sega, the Japanese video game manufacturer, joined forces with Williams-Renault in 1993. However, the day is still a long way off when drivers will be able to guide their cars remotely with video joy sticks.

TRACTION CONTROL
Controls traction under acceleration by delivering power progressively to the wheels

ELECTRONIC AIDS
Six 'driver aids' have contributed to improving the performance of Formula 1 cars.

1989: NEAR REVOLUTION IN GEARBOX TECHNOLOGY
The 1989 Brazilian Grand Prix will be remembered in the history of Formula 1 as the first race to be won by a car fitted with a semi-automatic gearbox. Using a system devised by John Barnard, Nigel Mansell did not need to take his hands off the wheel at any stage of the race. Moving up and down the gears became a simple matter of flicking one of two switches located to the left and right on the reverse side of the steering wheel. This electro-pneumatic system was soon taken up by all the top teams, including Williams-Renault and McLaren.

POWER THROTTLE
Enables power to be transmitted progressively to the wheels as well as controlling engine speed during gear changes and when idling

FIGHTER-PILOT VISION

When consulting his instruments, a driver takes his eyes off the track for approximately one second at a time. To eliminate this hindrance, British company Frazer-Nash and the French group 'Aérospatiale' are currently exploring adapting 'head-up display' helmets of the type worn by helicopter combat pilots to a use in Formula 1. Information appears momentarily or permanently on a tiny display situated in the line of sight.

DRIVER VERSUS CHIP

Drivers all agree that electronic aids will never replace talent. At most, they concede that they could reduce the performance gap between cars. However, it is still the person behind the wheel who makes the real difference. Despite what might commonly be believed, a highly electronic car demands a great deal more mental effort from the driver than does a 'conventional' car, and setting up has become something of a Chinese puzzle. Alain Prost, arguably the best development driver in the sport, frequently admitted to having major difficulties understanding his car.

HEAD-UP DISPLAY HELMET
The five red lights tell the driver he is in 5th. When revs reach 12,500 rpm, a grey light indicates it is time to change up to 6th gear…

…In third gear at 9,000 rpm, the red light has just come on to warn of a major engine or chassis problem necessitating an immediate stop

DRIVER'S EYE VIEW OF THE HEAD-UP DISPLAY HELMET

ACTIVE SUSPENSION
Allows ride height to adjust in real time to the track's profile and to the car's aerodynamics

TELEMETRY
Telemetry permanently transmits information concerning the engine and chassis to engineers

A SPY IN THE CAB

Thanks to dozens of sensors located at strategic points in the car, data is transmitted to the pits either in real time or each time it passes the pits, enabling engineers to keep a constant watch on the chassis and engine.

Safety in Formula 1

As top speeds of F1 cars have risen, driver safety has become an increasing priority and many new regulations have come into force. Measures such as making sure that new pedals are located behind the centre line of the front wheels, for example, have left legs far less prone to danger in case of frontal impact. A carbon and "Kevlar" survival cell is capable of withstanding violent shocks that the human body could not survive. Fire remains a worrying concern, since the basic materials used in the construction of cars are so highly inflammable.

The roll-over bar prevents drivers being squashed in the event of a roll

SURVIVAL KIT
Driver safety is paramount, and a battery of mandatory FIA-approved equipment guarantees that drivers are afforded maximum protection in the event of a collision or fire. Scrutineers regularly check to see that this equipment is on board the cars.

In case of fire, an on-board oxygen bottle ensures roughly thirty seconds supply of breathable air. Very few drivers actually connect this system to their helmet

CRASHES
Should a driver lose control of his machine, it is preferable to try and swipe any obstacle sideways, or with the rear. The car can absorb energy more efficiently in this way. In case of frontal impact, drivers try to fold up their legs and crouch over in their seat. During the 1989 French Grand Prix, Mauricio Gugelmin had little time to think when a rival car climbed his rear wheel. The Brazilian happily escaped unhurt from the ensuing spectacular crash, and he was ready for the race's re-start.

Full-harness belts restrain the driver and prevent him from being ejected

NUMBER OF DRIVERS KILLED EACH DECADE

1950-59: 21
1960-69: 27
1970-79: 12
1980-89: 7
1990-93: 0

THE BATTLE HAS BEEN WON

Thankfully, the time has passed when F1 would lose two drivers a year. Today, death no longer stalks the circuits.

SEE AND BE SEEN

In the case of poor visibility, drivers must switch on a red light fitted at the rear of the car.

Moulded to match the shape of the driver's back, the carbon seat provides added protection in an accident by keeping the driver well inside the survival cell, essentially the central part of the chassis

To reduce the risk of fire, Formula 1 cars use deformable fuel tanks made from puncture-proof "Kevlar". All fuel lines are of the auto cut-off type in case of breakage and an extinguisher is plumbed into this 'sensitive' zone of the car

RESUSCITATION
I.V. FLUIDS
DRESSINGS
HYDRAULIC CUTTERS / SPREADERS

FORMULA 1 SAMARITANS

Ambulances and firefighting vehicles are located at strategic points around the circuit in order to be in action within seconds of any accident.

Official practice

DRIVERS PRACTICALLY SPEND THE ENTIRE TWO DAYS of official practice in conversation with their Team Director, engineers, mechanics, sponsors or journalists. Curiously, they spend precious little time in their cars, especially since new regulations introduced in 1993 set an upper limit on the number of laps each driver can put in. On average, a driver will spend just one hour actually behind the wheel on each of the two days of practice. On the other hand, in the privacy of his pits or motorhome, he will spend more than six hours a day in discussion with members of his team in an endeavour to find the best settings possible.

STARTING GRID
Official practice takes place on the Friday and Saturday preceding every Grand Prix. The timetable is always identical: 09.30-11.00 am free practice, 1:00-2:00 pm qualifying practice. Practice is vital since it dictates where on the grid a driver will start Sunday's race, positions depending on lap times set during the two official sessions. A poor grid position can be a big handicap since overtaking can be difficult in Formula 1.

6: Brundle, Ligier-Renault
1 min 22.421 sec

5: Patrese, Benetton-Ford
1 min 22.364 sec

4: Senna, McLaren-Ford
1 min 21.986 sec

3: Schumacher, Benetton-Ford
1 min 20.401 sec

2: Hill, Williams-Renault
1 min 19.134 sec

1: Prost, Williams-Renault
1 min 19.006 sec

1993 BRITISH GRAND PRIX

A DAY IN THE LIFE
The schedule for practice follows the same routine at every race. Whatever the circuit, drivers always observe the same ritual, arriving at the track, taking lunch and holding technical briefings at the same time each day. Every second is committed to improving the cars' performance.

CHANGING ROOM
Drivers change into racing overalls inside the team's transporter. Gloves and helmet will be put on just before climbing into the car. As a general rule, drivers leave the transport of gear such as overalls, shoes and gloves to the team. However, they entrust no-one with the task of looking after their helmet

AUTOGRAPH HUNTERS
Entry to the paddock is strictly controlled. However, determined spectators occasionally succeed in slipping through the net. They are willing to wait for hours by the gate in the hope of getting an autograph

ARRIVAL AT THE CIRCUIT
Drivers get to the circuit at around 8 am. If the team has the means, and if traffic is congested, they might arrive by helicopter. More usually however, they arrive by car. A special car park is provided for them close to the paddock

BASIC SETTINGS
Once kitted up, the first priority is to talk with engineers about the car's basic settings, selected according to the type of circuit. A programme of work is established for the free practice session

Pie chart labels

FIA administrative obligations: 15 mins

Public Relations: 2 hours

Transport: 1 hour

Relaxation: 30 mins

Sleep: 8½ hours

Technical briefings: 6¼ hours

Massage: 30 mins

Driving: 1 hour

Interviews: 2 hours

Meals: 2 hours

INTERVIEWS

Something like 600 media representatives attend each Grand Prix, and drivers will spend an average of two hours every day with journalists. This can take the form of individual interviews or press conferences. The drivers most in demand are those who set the best qualifying times.

24 HOURS IN THE LIFE OF A FORMULA 1 DRIVER

Around six hours are spent discussing the setting up of the car, compared with just one hour behind the wheel. This may seem disproportionate, but such meetings can have an important bearing on the final outcome of the race.

SECOND BITE

After using their first set of tyres, drivers stop to fit fresh rubber, fine-tune settings and catch up on how rivals are faring. At the same time, they will be looking for a moment when the track is relatively clear of traffic to go out for a second attempt

THE MEDIA

Practice has just finished and, as he climbs out of his car, Alain Prost is surrounded by the press. In general, he will give them around fifteen minutes of his time. According to whom he is addressing, Prost, like Ayrton Senna, can switch effortlessly to any one of three languages which, in the Frenchman's case, are French, English and Italian

QUALIFYING PRACTICE

Drivers have one hour, twelve laps and two sets of tyres to try and set the fastest lap time possible

POLE POSITION

Alain Prost waves to the public. He has just set the fastest time of the day and will therefore start the next day's race from pole position, the most coveted place on the grid. His performance also means additional work: the fastest driver in practice must go directly to the media room for a press conference before being able to return to his motorhome for a de-briefing session with his engineers

LUNCH

Between free practice and qualifying practice, drivers have two hours at their disposal to reflect on the best settings for their cars and take a light lunch in the team's motorhome

FREE PRACTICE

Drivers have a maximum of 23 laps during Friday and Saturday's free practice to set up their cars with full fuel tanks. They will also test with empty tanks in order to have the best chance of setting a blistering lap time during the afternoon's qualifying session

MOTORHOMES

Each team has its own luxury motorhome in the paddock. This is where drivers retire to eat or be massaged, whilst Team Directors profit from its privacy to entertain VIP guests or negotiate future contracts. It is also here that mechanics will take their evening meal at the end of the day when all at the circuit is calm.

The media and Formula 1

FORMULA 1 IS ONE OF THE SPORTS that generate the greatest amount of media coverage in the world. The number of journalists following F1 – barely a handful in 1950 when the World Championship was created – has literally gone through the ceiling. Today, the sport is covered by something like 6,000 reporters representing forty different countries and all types of media. Beforehand, however, they must have applied for special authorization from the FIA to obtain the necessary access passes into circuits. TV companies must pay special broadcasting rights.

TRULY INTERNATIONAL
In the press office of a Formula 1 Grand Prix, you stand to hear nearly every language spoken in the world. Journalists begin to arrive at the circuit on the Thursday prior to the first day of official practice. Facilities at their disposal include full television coverage of the race, as well as monitors providing lap-by-lap times and overall positions.

TV reporter

PRESS CONFERENCES
To simplify the media's task, official press conferences provide an opportunity to question the drivers in the top three positions on the Saturday afternoon and, on the Sunday, minutes after the flag, the top three finishers of the Grand Prix itself.

GLOBAL TV COVERAGE
Live satellite transmission of races has turned Formula 1 into a truly global sport covering all five continents. A total audience of thirty billion viewers is estimated to have followed the 1993 World Championship from their armchairs. Broadcasting rights are the property of the Formula 1 Constructors' Association (FOCA), which handles their sale to individual TV companies. No professional cameraman is able to gain access to a circuit unless his camera sports the special sticker certifying that he has already obtained the necessary authorization to film.

Cameraman

46

HUNGRY FOR INFORMATION
On the grid, during the minutes leading up to the start, it is easy to spot the most popular drivers by the number of reporters standing by their cars. These journalists wait to record the last-minute thoughts and quotes of the stars at the front of the grid.

Television sound engineer

Radio reporter

Reporter

NUMBER OF JOURNALISTS ACCREDITED FOR SELECTED TOP SPORTING EVENTS

Football World Cup: 7,000

A season of Formula 1: 6,000

America's Cup: 2,200

Roland Garros: 1,200

Tour de France: 900

JOURNALISTS IN THEIR THOUSANDS
Formula 1 is one of the sports that receive the most media coverage in the world. In 1993, no less than 6,000 photographers and newspaper, radio and TV correspondents were accredited by the Fédération Internationale de l'Automobile to cover the F1 World Championship.

TONS OF PAPER
Each Grand Prix generates a huge amount of written information. On the photo front, in order to meet tight deadlines, certain magazines supply their photographers with special machines that analyse photos numerically. These pictures, like written articles, can then be transmitted directly to editorial desks around the world by telephone.

SHOOTING FILM
An average of two hundred photographers are present at any one Grand Prix. In the space of three days, they will take something like 1,000 frames each, often processing them on-site before electronically transmitting them across the globe.

A Grand Prix start

THE SECONDS IMMEDIATELY BEFORE THE START, as cars take up position on the grid after the formation lap, are the most intense moment of a Grand Prix. Despite the clamour of the engines, all seems silent, a silence that only serves to accentuate the thunderous climax of the start itself. The two drivers on the front row have clear asphalt ahead. In the distance, they see the first corner, the first braking point. Those behind see just an abstract mass of tyres and rear wings. It is through this wall that they must attempt to pick out a path when the green light comes on, even if that means wheel-to-wheel contact with other cars.

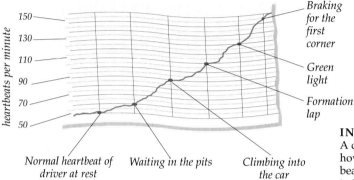

heartbeats per minute

150
130
110
90
70
50

Braking for the first corner

Green light

Formation lap

Normal heartbeat of driver at rest

Waiting in the pits

Climbing into the car

CONCENTRATION
Drivers' reactions when the light switches to green are on a par with those of a 100-metre sprinter as the starting pistol is fired – something in the order of a few hundredths of a second! The instant a driver lowers his visor, his thoughts are already elsewhere. Nothing else exists. The race has already begun.

INCREASING HEARTBEAT
A driver's heartbeat underlines how intense the start is. From 50 beats a minute, the figure rockets to 150 braking for the first corner

N° 2
Cars pull up at their allotted place on the grid. As they do so, a marshal (one per car) lowers the board bearing the driver's number

5"
Once all boards are lowered, the starter shows the 5-second board. The red light will come on within the next five seconds

When the red light shows, drivers know the start will be given within between four and seven seconds

Yellow light: an incident – a stalled engine perhaps – has interrupted the start. A slow lap is completed before drivers take up position again

The green light flashes on and twenty six drivers put their foot to the floor simultaneously. The Grand Prix has started

THE STARTING GRID
From first to last, the position of drivers on the grid is a function of the best personal time set during the two qualifying practice sessions. A painted mark indicates the spot where cars should stop. To reduce the risk of tangles, the grid is staggered and two cars on the same row are separated by a distance of four metres. An eight-metre gap separates cars lined up on either side of the track.

The reward for being fastest in qualifying practice is pole position, the inside slot on the front row

Formula 1 cars take to the track to complete a reconnaissance lap before taking up their place on the grid

The pit-lane has been closed. Any car remaining in its pits can still start the race, but from a position at the rear of the grid

The grid is cleared. Only the driver, his car and his mechanics may remain

Engines start and it is now the mechanics' turn to leave the track

Within thirty seconds of this board being shown, a green flag at the front of the grid will wave cars off for the formation lap

Cars set off for the formation lap before taking up position again on the grid, engines running

COUNTDOWN

Start procedure begins thirty minutes before the scheduled start as cars join the track for one or more reconnaissance laps. Those opting for more than one lap must pass via the pit-lane at reduced speed each time. Once cars are in position on the grid, the countdown starts. Certain drivers stay in their cars, helmets on, motionless. Others prefer to stretch their legs and chat, helmets off. Progressively, the grid clears and engines fire up. The drivers are on their own as they wait for the formation lap to start.

THE MOMENT OF RISK

Drivers know perfectly well that the best chance of making up a few places is between the start-line and the moment the cars start braking for the first corner. Those in front generally succeed in squeezing through. Behind, however, wheel-to-wheel dicing and a tendency to bottleneck make this one of the riskiest moments of the entire race.

WHEELSPIN

Caused by accelerating too hard or letting out the clutch too briskly, wheelspin is what drivers dread the most as the light turns to green. Rear wheels, unable to transmit all the power effectively, spin helplessly. Drivers stand to lose a few places if this happens to them.

OTHER TYPES OF START

The traditional Le Mans start (left) involved drivers running across the track and jumping into their cars. Spectacular but unsafe. It was replaced in 1969 by a 'rolling start' behind an official pace-car which dives to one side as it crosses the start-line. This system is also used in Indy racing (right).

POLE POSITION

Ayrton Senna has started from pole position no fewer than sixty two times, an outright record. And, at the age of just 33, it is exceedingly likely he will add to that figure. Nonetheless, Senna has recently lost two personal records; the number of pole positions obtained in a single season – beaten by Mansell in 1992 (fourteen) – and the number of consecutive pole positions in a single season – beaten by Prost in 1993 (seven).

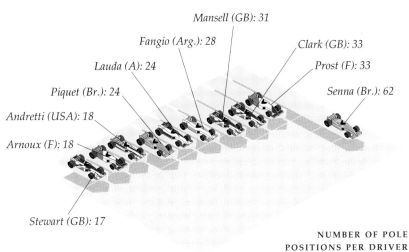

Mansell (GB): 31
Fangio (Arg.): 28
Clark (GB): 33
Lauda (A): 24
Prost (F): 33
Piquet (Br.): 24
Senna (Br.): 62
Andretti (USA): 18
Arnoux (F): 18
Stewart (GB): 17

NUMBER OF POLE
POSITIONS PER DRIVER

The race

THE HIGHLIGHT OF THE GRAND PRIX WEEKEND is, of course, the race. The instant the light turns green, twenty six highly determined drivers are literally unleashed. For the driver in front, his immediate task is to build up his lead and ward off the pressure of his pursuers. For those caught up in the pack, the job is doubly difficult. Along every straight, through every corner, their sole objective is to carve a way through the field. Overtaking is the name of the game, moving up the leaderboard to finish in the highest position possible.

1950:
2h 40min
408km

1960:
2h 18min
392km

1970:
1h 45min
336km

1980:
1h 38min
305km

1990:
1h 24min
299km

SHORT AND ACTION-PACKED
Since the creation of Formula 1, both the duration of races and the distances involved have shortened considerably. Today's races last little more than half the time taken for a Grand Prix in the 1950s. TV, which prefers short, action-filled races, is the principal reason for this trend.

OVERTAKING TECHNIQUES

LATE BRAKING
The driver of the white car has out-braked his rival on the inside line. He is therefore able to turn-in earlier and accelerate out of the corner in front. A text-book manoeuvre

SLIPSTREAMING
The driver of the white car is less affected by aerodynamic turbulence. As he pulls out to overtake, he benefits from an added turn of speed to pass and pull clear

OVERTAKING AT MONZA AND MONACO
Racing is all about overtaking. Unfortunately, the layout of certain circuits can make this a very complicated task indeed. The ideal place is at the end of a long straight preceding a reasonably tight corner. This gives the braver drivers a chance to out-brake their rivals. Monza boasts a number of such places. At the other end of the scale, the absence of straights around Monaco's narrow, cambered street-circuit makes overtaking all but impossible. An eloquent example was Mansell's duel with Senna there in 1992. Despite being four seconds a lap quicker than the Brazilian, the Williams-Renault driver eventually had to give up trying to get past and settle for second.

Monza

Monaco

THE MOST GRAND PRIX STARTS (TEAMS)

Ferrari 521 Grand Prix	Lotus 474	Brabham 394	McLaren 394	Tyrrell 328	Williams 313	Ligier 277	March 200	Arrows 197	BRM 197

THE MOST GRAND PRIX STARTS (DRIVERS)

Patrese (I) 256 Grand Prix	Piquet (Br) 204	Prost (F) 199	de Cesaris (I) 197	Mansell (GB) 181	Alboreto (I) 178	Laffite (F) 176	G Hill (GB) 176	Lauda (A) 171

Prost's pit-board was identified by a French flag

The word "Tyres" indicates that mechanics are prepared for a tyre change

TYRES
P|1
DAMON ▮-4

GETTING THE MESSAGE

The quality of radio contact with drivers is not always crystal sharp. Pit-boards are therefore used to confirm important messages each time a driver passes his pits. In this picture, the Williams-Renault team informs Alain Prost that he is leading Damon Hill by four seconds and that new tyres are ready if required.

DRINK AND DRIVE

Drivers often carry a refreshment inside a collapsible bottle located either in the cockpit, in the side pods, in the nose cone or even against the driver's chest. He quenches his thirst either by sucking at a tube or by activating a small electrical pump.

Pit stops

IN THE COURSE OF MOST RACES, cars will make at least one mid-race stop at their pits in order to change tyres. Varying weather conditions can even result in cars making a number of such stops. To ensure that this operation passes off with minimum time loss, regular dress rehearsals are held. Each mechanic knows his individual role by heart and his movements eventually become automatic reflexes. The swiftness of this operation can occasionally mean the difference between first and second place, so this is no job for fumblers.

ALL FOR ONE
A tyre change requires fifteen mechanics – three to remove and replace each wheel, two on the quick-lift jacks, and the chief mechanic who holds the "lollipop". These may be joined by one to clean the driver's visor and another to steady the car.

QUICK-LIFT JACKS
Before tyres can be changed, the car first needs to be lifted off the ground. A mechanical jack would be far too slow for this job. Instead, a 'quick-lift' jack is used. The mechanic wheels it into position before applying all his weight to the other end to lift the car. At the front, some teams prefer air-jacks, which are quicker and give drivers a better idea of the exact spot where they should stop.

AIR-POWER: THE ULTIMATE WEAPON
The wheels of Formula 1 cars are tightened with a single central wheelnut. To unscrew it and re-tighten it after a change, mechanics use air-tools powered by bottles of compressed air located in the pits.

EARLY MORNING PRACTICE
To ensure that tyre changes are completed as swiftly as possible, mechanics often train early in the morning before practice or before private test-sessions. This sort of exercise is likely to become more common with the introduction of mid-race refuelling in 1994.

REFLEX WORK
Mechanics have been known to change all four tyres in less than five seconds. Delays can cost a driver victory. Perhaps the best known example was Mansell losing his wheel in the pit-lane at Estoril in 1991

TYRE-CHANGE TIMES
1993 BRITISH GRAND PRIX

Seconds 1 2 3 4 5 6 7 8 9

McLaren: 5.11s (Senna)

Benetton: 5.50s (Schumacher)

Ligier: 6.75s (Brundle)

Williams: 7.61s (Hill)

Williams: 8.02s (Prost)

Lotus: 9.21s (Zanardi)

MECHANICS TAKE UP POSITION
The moment to change tyres has been agreed

THE CAR ARRIVES
Jacks lift the car as wheelnuts are untightened

THE "LOLLIPOP"
The board held up by the Chief Mechanic in front of the car has affectionately become known as the "lollipop". It either informs the driver that he must keep his foot on the brakes ("Brakes on") or that he is free to drive off ("Go")

THE WHEELS COME OFF
New wheels and tyres are fitted as the old ones are jettisoned towards the pits

A RISK OF THE JOB
Despite the fact that gloves are worn for wheel changes, it is not uncommon for mechanics to slightly burn their hands by accidently touching the brake calipers, wheels or tyres – all of which are at their maximum temperature

TIGHTENING
The driver has his foot on the brakes as the mechanics tighten the wheelnuts

SPARE TOOLS
In case of a problem, spare air-guns are positioned around the car within easy reach of mechanics. Each crew also has a spare wheelnut in case the one on the car proves too damaged for re-use, a reasonably frequent occurrence

TYRE-MEN
Two mechanics are responsible for checking the new tyres, which are kept ready in warmers at the back of the pits before being passed to the mechanics posted in the pit-lane

THE MECHANICS STAND CLEAR
The mechanics lift their arms, the jacks come down and the car races off

Forced out

Being forced to retire from a race is probably the worst form of defeat for a driver, since it means he is unable to defend his chances right up to the flag. Over the years, technological progress has tended to reduce the proportion of retirements due to mechanical failures. However, the number of 'driver-related' retirements, such as collisions or going off the track, is on the increase. Not that today's drivers are any less skillful. It's simply that cars are now so close in terms of performance, and braking distances have become so short, that drivers must take more risks if they want to move up a notch in practice or during a race.

CLUTCH
A poor start or a spin might lead a driver to ask too much of his clutch. Excessive clutch slip causes the carbon clutch plate to over-heat and this in turn can result in the clutch hub's splines sheering off, spelling instant retirement.

ENGINE
Engine failure results from one of three reasons – a broken internal component, excessive oil consumption, or blocked side pods that cause over-heating. The first is the most spectacular. The part that breaks very often puts a hole in the sump, and the consequent loss of oil causes a tremendous cloud of smoke. The advent of semi-automatic gearboxes has all but eliminated engine failure caused by over-revving.

GEARBOX AND TRANSMISSION
A return to reasonable levels of power has reduced the number of transmission failures, which used to be frequent in the days of the turbo. Considerable ongoing work goes into reducing the weight of the gearbox, but gears and shift-forks do not always stand up to such slimming exercises.

COLLISIONS: WHOSE FAULT IS IT?

SPIN
Spins are caused by a sudden loss of grip of the rear wheels, due either to braking too late or accelerating too early. A spin does not necessarily spell retirement from a race. That is unless the engine stalls, or unless the car ends up stranded in a sand-trap.

The car behind has not succeeded in gaining the advantage by late braking

The leading car can therefore pursue its normal line

THE ASSAILANT IN THE WRONG
The driver of the second car attempts to pass on the inside but hasn't gained sufficient advantage by braking late. The driver in front has every right to continue on his ideal line. However, the front wheel of the second car touches the rear wheel of the car it is attempting to pass. Responsibility lies with the assailant who should have backed off.

CAUSES OF RETIREMENT

1992: 416 starts, 211 retirements

- Miscellaneous: 15 (7%)
- Electrical: 9 (4%)
- Clutch: 11 (5%)
- Accidents: 31 (15%)
- Gearbox & transmission: 42 (20%)
- Collisions: 45 (21%)
- Engine: 58 (28%)

Accidents and collisions today account for 49% of all retirements in F1. The same figure in 1960, when engine and gearbox failures were each responsible for a third of retirements, was 15%

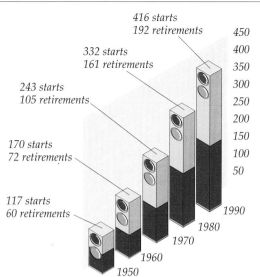

- 416 starts / 192 retirements — 1990
- 332 starts / 161 retirements — 1980
- 243 starts / 105 retirements — 1970
- 170 starts / 72 retirements — 1960
- 117 starts / 60 retirements — 1950

ELECTRICAL FAILURE
'Electrical failures' sometimes provide a handy excuse when a team either doesn't know the real reason for a problem or else doesn't want it to be known. Even so, a severed wire, a faulty coil, a malfunction on one of the electronic management packs or an alternator failure can effectively cause an engine to stop.

HOW THE RELIABILITY OF FORMULA 1 CARS HAS EVOLVED
There are more retirements in F1 today than in the 1960s. However, there are fewer mechanical failures, whilst collisions and accidents are on the increase.

PUNCTURES
The usual cause of a puncture in Formula 1 is driving over debris – left on the track after a collision, for example. Air loss from the tyre is slow, and drivers generally have sufficient time to reach their pits to fit fresh tyres. A tyre that is worn, however, can sometimes explode, and this means instant retirement. This is what happened to Damon Hill two laps from the finish of the 1993 German Grand Prix when victory seemed in the bag.

COLLISIONS
Whilst the reliability of Formula 1 cars continues to improve, the same cannot be said of drivers. Collisions, a rare occurrence in the 1950s and 60s, are today the second most common cause of retirement. Excessive driver optimism is not the only reason for this. The growing number of collisions is a clear indication that overtaking, the whole point of racing, has become extremely difficult in Formula 1.

GOING OFF
In wet weather, grip is low and the number of spins and cars leaving the track tends to rise. Drivers generally don't like admitting it was their fault when they find themselves 'parked' off the track. In their defence, mechanical problems or patches of oil not signaled by marshals are responsible for one accident in two.

The front wheels of the chasing car tangle with the rear wheels of the car in front

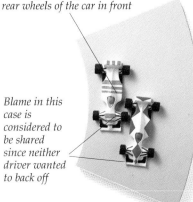

Blame in this case is considered to be shared since neither driver wanted to back off

SHARED RESPONSIBILITY
The second car has stolen half a length by out-braking his rival. Although on the inside, his advantage still isn't sufficient to allow him to turn in first. The driver in front wants to prove a point and stays on his ideal line. As neither is prepared to back off, responsibility is considered shared.

The chasing driver has succeeded in pulling alongside

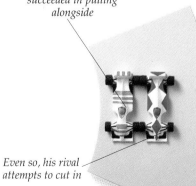

Even so, his rival attempts to cut in

THE DEFENDER IN THE WRONG
In this case, the chasing driver has succeeded in drawing level with his rival as they prepare to turn-in. Since he is on the inside, he is well placed to steer into the corner first. However, the leading driver refuses to give way, and front and rear wheels touch. The driver trying to defend his position is in the wrong.

Victory!

OF THE 543 DRIVERS WHO HAVE RACED in F1 since 1950, 124 have scored World Championship points. However, only 70 belong to the elite club of past Grand Prix winners. Of these, 17 can lay claim to just one success. Most of these one-off results can be explained either by a stroke of good fortune on the day or because the drivers in question sadly lost their lives just as their careers were taking off. Musso, Bandini, Cevert, Nilsson, Pace, for example. Two drivers who amply deserved to win – but didn't – were New Zealander Chris Amon and France's Jean-Pierre Jarier. During his career, Amon covered a distance of nearly 800 km in front – the equivalent of three Grands Prix – without ever succeeding in being first across the line, often falling foul of some mechanical problem with the flag in sight. British driver Peter Gethin was significantly more fortunate. In his entire career, he spent just 11 kilometres up front. That was sufficient for him to clinch the Italian Grand Prix in 1971.

THE CHEQUERED FLAG
The points system used in Formula 1 is 10 points for the winner, 6 points for second place, 4 for third, 3 for fourth, 2 for fifth and 1 for sixth. Drivers finishing further down than sixth do not score points. If a race is stopped before 75% of its scheduled distance has been covered (rain, accident), only half the points are awarded. In the World Constructors' Championship, points are awarded in the same manner, teams totalling the scores of both cars.

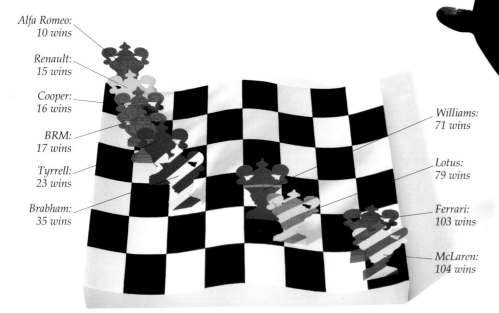

Alfa Romeo: 10 wins
Renault: 15 wins
Cooper: 16 wins
BRM: 17 wins
Tyrrell: 23 wins
Brabham: 35 wins

Williams: 71 wins
Lotus: 79 wins
Ferrari: 103 wins
McLaren: 104 wins

NUMBER OF WINS PER TEAM
McLaren started in F1 sixteen years after Ferrari but has today pulled ahead of the 'Scuderia' in the wins table, thanks to its domination at the end of the 1980s. Since 1992, McLaren has fallen back slightly, its place taken up by Williams, Champion in 1992 and 1993.

PROST'S RECORD
With a total of 51 wins, Alain Prost holds the record for the most wins in F1. His most pressing challenger is Ayrton Senna, five years his junior. The Brazilian's career will also continue, unlike that of Prost, who retired in 1993.

PODIUM

The record for the most wins in a single season belongs to Nigel Mansell. The British driver was first past the flag on no fewer than nine occasions in 1992. Previous holder of the record had been Ayrton Senna who took eight wins in 1988.

Great Britain: 150 wins (28%) 13 drivers

Brazil: 79 wins (15%) 4 drivers

France: 77 wins (15%) 10 drivers

Austria: 39 wins (7%) 3 drivers

Italy: 39 wins (7%) 13 drivers

Argentina: 38 wins (7%) 3 drivers

Australia: 26 wins (5%) 2 drivers

USA: 22 wins (4%) 5 drivers

Sweden: 12 wins (2%) 3 drivers

New Zealand: 12 wins (2%) 2 drivers

Belgium: 11 wins (2%) 2 drivers

Germany, South Africa, Switzerland, Canada, Mexico, Finland: 35 wins (6%) 9 drivers

WINS BY NATIONALITY

In terms of Grand Prix wins, Great Britain is Formula 1's most successful nation. Brazil, thanks to its three World Champions (Senna , Piquet and Fittipaldi), is equal second with France, a country that owes two-thirds of its victories to just one man – Alain Prost. Italy, the second most prolific supplier of drivers to Grand Prix racing after Great Britain, ranks but fourth. Four countries have produced only one Grand Prix winner: Finland, Canada, South Africa and Mexico.

YOUNGEST

Bruce McLaren became the youngest winner in F1's history by winning the 1959 USA Grand Prix at the age of 22.

OLDEST

First past the flag in the 1951 French Grand Prix at the age of 53, Luigi Fagioli remains Formula 1's oldest ever winner.

OUT OF CONTROL

Taking the flag for the only F1 win of his career (Austria, 1975), Vittorio Brambilla lifted his arms in anticipation to show his joy. He promptly lost control of his car and smashed into the rails!

CLOSEST FINISH

Peter Gethin headed Ronnie Peterson across the line of the 1971 Italian Grand Prix by just one hundredth of a second, the closest ever finish recorded in Formula 1.

PERSEVERANCE

Andrea de Cesaris is without doubt F1's most persevering driver. From 197 starts, the Italian has never won a race!

NUMBER OF WINS PER DRIVER

41 Senna (Br.)

27 Stewart (GB)

24 Fangio (Arg.)

16 Moss (GB)

51 Prost (F)

30 Mansell (GB)

25 Lauda (A) Clark (GB)

23 Piquet (Br.)

14 Brabham (Aus.)

World Champions

THE FORMULA 1 WORLD CHAMPIONSHIP, motor racing's most coveted accolade, is awarded to the driver who scores the most points in the course of a season. Since 1950, twenty three different drivers have taken the crown. Some, like Fangio, have won it as many as three, four or five times. Certain drivers succeeded in clinching the title despite winning just one race in the course of the season, whilst Mansell was first past the flag nine times in his championship-winning year. The question regularly arises as to just who is the Champion of all Champions. Whilst this particular debate is never likely to be definitively resolved, four drivers have tended to stand out in the history of Formula 1. In order of appearance, they are Fangio, Clark, Prost and Senna.

JOCHEN RINDT
Jochen Rindt had promised his wife Nina that once he had won the world title, he would retire from Formula 1. As fate had it, he was killed at Monza in 1970 and awarded the crown posthumously.

JOHN SURTEES
Six-times 500 cc motorbike Champion, John Surtees also won the world Formula 1 crown in 1964. His feat of taking the title on both two and four wheels – at the highest level possible – is unlikely to be repeated.

PROST: FOUR WORLD TITLES
For a long time, Juan Manuel Fangio's record of five world titles looked unbeatable. Then Alain Prost and Ayrton Senna arived on the scene. In 1993, Prost won his fourth world crown before retiring from Formula 1 which leaves Ayrton Senna, three times World Champion, as the only driver with a real chance of joining Fangio at the summit in the foreseeable future.

JIM CLARK
Perhaps the greatest of them all. Two world titles and 25 F1 wins barely do justice to his talent. He was killed in the prime of his career, aged 32, during a race of secondary importance one wet Sunday afternoon at Hockenheim.

JACKIE STEWART
Three-times World Champion, Jackie Stewart actively contributed to bringing F1 into its modern era by campaigning to improve driver safety. Today, F1 drivers no longer die at the wheel. Perhaps that's his greatest triumph.

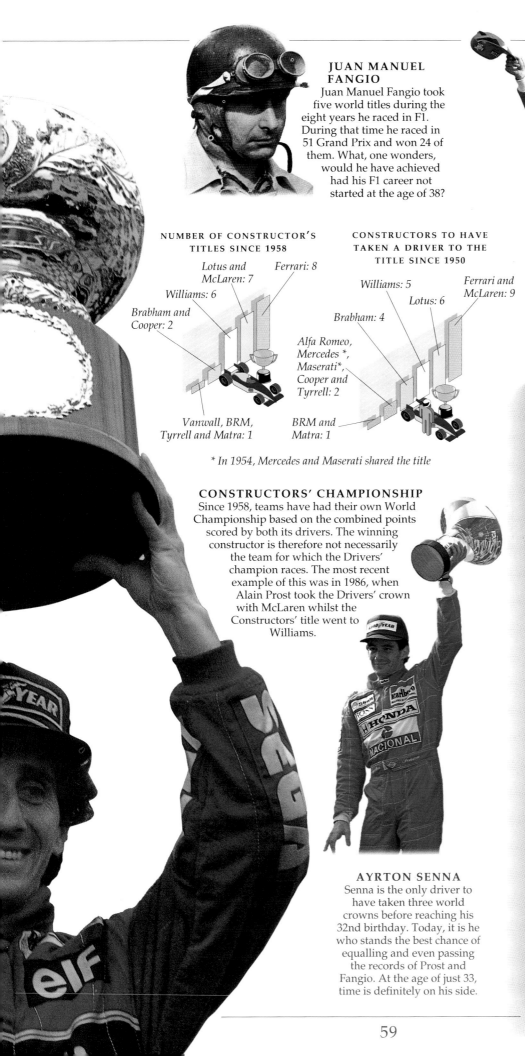

JUAN MANUEL FANGIO

Juan Manuel Fangio took five world titles during the eight years he raced in F1. During that time he raced in 51 Grand Prix and won 24 of them. What, one wonders, would he have achieved had his F1 career not started at the age of 38?

NIKI LAUDA

Niki Lauda twice 'retired' from F1, the first time after a particularly close shave with death, the second because he was beginning to feel bored with the sport. On both occasions, he came back to add a further world title to his personal record.

NUMBER OF CONSTRUCTOR'S TITLES SINCE 1958

Lotus and McLaren: 7
Ferrari: 8
Williams: 6
Brabham and Cooper: 2
Vanwall, BRM, Tyrrell and Matra: 1

CONSTRUCTORS TO HAVE TAKEN A DRIVER TO THE TITLE SINCE 1950

Williams: 5
Ferrari and McLaren: 9
Lotus: 6
Brabham: 4
Alfa Romeo, Mercedes *, Maserati*, Cooper and Tyrrell: 2
BRM and Matra: 1

In 1954, Mercedes and Maserati shared the title

CONSTRUCTORS' CHAMPIONSHIP

Since 1958, teams have had their own World Championship based on the combined points scored by both its drivers. The winning constructor is therefore not necessarily the team for which the Drivers' champion races. The most recent example of this was in 1986, when Alain Prost took the Drivers' crown with McLaren whilst the Constructors' title went to Williams.

AYRTON SENNA

Senna is the only driver to have taken three world crowns before reaching his 32nd birthday. Today, it is he who stands the best chance of equalling and even passing the records of Prost and Fangio. At the age of just 33, time is definitely on his side.

WORLD F1 DRIVERS' CHAMPIONS (1950-1993)		
1950	Farina (I)	Alfa Romeo
1951	Fangio (Arg.)	Alfa Romeo
1952	Ascari (I)	Ferrari
1953	Ascari (I)	Ferrari
1954	Fangio (Arg.)	Mercedes & Maserati
1955	Fangio (Arg.)	Mercedes
1956	Fangio (Arg.)	Lancia & Ferrari
1957	Fangio (Arg.)	Maserati
1958	Hawthorn (GB)	Ferrari
1959	Brabham (Aus.)	Cooper-Climax
1960	Brabham (Aus.)	Cooper-Climax
1961	P Hill (USA)	Ferrari
1962	G Hill (GB)	BRM
1963	Clark (GB)	Lotus-Climax
1964	John Surtees (GB)	Ferrari
1965	Clark (GB)	Lotus-Climax
1966	Brabham (Aus.)	Brabham-Repco
1967	Hulme (NZ)	Brabham-Repco
1968	G Hill (GB)	Lotus-Ford
1969	Stewart (GB)	Matra-Ford
1970	Rindt (A)	Lotus-Ford
1971	Stewart (GB)	Tyrrell-Ford
1972	Fittipaldi (Br.)	Lotus-Ford
1973	Stewart (GB)	Tyrrell-Ford
1974	Fittipaldi (Br.)	McLaren-Ford
1975	Lauda (A)	Ferrari
1976	Hunt (GB)	McLaren-Ford
1977	Lauda (A)	Ferrari
1978	Andretti (USA)	Lotus-Ford
1979	Scheckter (SA)	Ferrari
1980	Jones (Aus.)	Williams-Ford
1981	Piquet (Br.)	Brabham-Ford
1982	Rosberg (Fin)	Williams-Ford
1983	Piquet (Br.)	Brabham BMW
1984	Lauda (A)	McLaren-Porsche
1985	Prost (F)	McLaren-Porsche
1986	Prost (F)	McLaren-Porsche
1987	Piquet (Br.)	Williams-Honda
1988	Senna (Br.)	McLaren-Honda
1989	Prost (F)	Mclaren-Honda
1990	Senna (Br.)	McLaren-Honda
1991	Senna (Br.)	McLaren-Honda
1992	Mansell (GB)	Williams-Renault
1993	Prost (F)	Williams-Renault

On to the next race

THE RACE HAS FINISHED and the clamour of the engines has faded, but another race is already under way. This one is against the clock, for teams always like to have as much time as possible to prepare for the following Grand Prix. Drivers are the first to leave, some at the controls of personal planes. At the nearest international airport, another plane is preparing for an 8 o'clock take-off with mechanics and engineers on-board. Two hours after the chequered flag has dropped, the hurriedly-loaded trucks finally get away. The aim is for personnel and equipment to be back at the factory on the Monday morning. For drivers, Monday is a day of rest. Private testing never begins before the Tuesday!

Kyalami, South Africa: 18,000 km return trip

São Paulo, Brazil: 20,000 km return trip

Donington, Great Britain: 400 km return trip

Imola, Italy: 2,600 km return trip

Barcelona, Spain: 3,000 km return trip

Monte-Carlo, Monaco: 2,400 km return trip

Montreal, Canada: 12,000 km return trip

Magny-Cours, France: 1,400 km return trip

Silverstone, Great Britain: 140 km return trip

Hockenheim, Germany: 2,000 km return trip

A RACE AROUND THE WORLD

Transporter trucks make their way back to base as quickly as possible after the finish of a Grand Prix. The sooner they get back, the better the team is able to prepare for the following Grand Prix. On a European scale, Renault Sport's Viry-Châtillon premises in the Paris suburbs are more centrally located than the Williams factory in Didcot, which is some 100 km north-west of London. Silverstone, just 70 km from Didcot, is the Williams team's home Grand Prix. The furthest afield is Adelaide. Having left a month beforehand for the Japanese Grand Prix, cars return to the UK a week after the Australian round having been shipped directly from Suzuka to the South Australian capital. This time, however, the work schedule is more relaxed, for Adelaide is the final Grand Prix of the season. The next world tour doesn't begin until after the winter-break.

THOROUGH CHECK-UP

Cars return to the factory on the Monday or the Tuesday after a Grand Prix. This leaves mechanics just a few days – a week at most during the European 'summer campaign' – to prepare for the following race. Before any revisions are made to the car's specification, a systematic six-point check is carried out.

STRIPPING THE CAR
Stripping the car takes half a day and allows mechanics to inspect parts and remove stones and rubber encrusted in the chassis

ENGINE CHANGE
The first task awaiting mechanics when cars get back to the factory is to remove the engines from the chassis in order to ship them back to the engine supplier

GEARBOX REVISION
Formula 1 gearboxes are systematically rebuilt after every race. The bevel gears are inspected for wear whilst gears, shift-forks and dog clutch are always changed

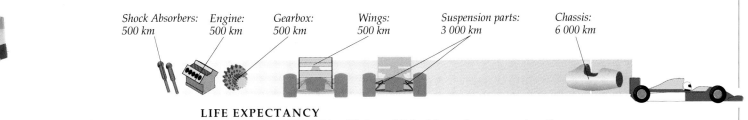

| Shock Absorbers: 500 km | Engine: 500 km | Gearbox: 500 km | Wings: 500 km | Suspension parts: 3 000 km | Chassis: 6 000 km |

LIFE EXPECTANCY

An estimated useful working life is established for each component on the car. As a precautionary measure, even if no sign of wear can be detected, parts are automatically replaced once this distance has been reached.

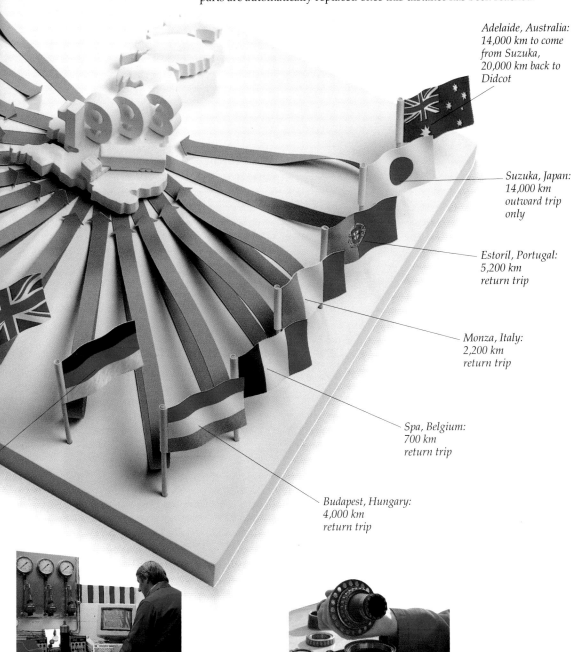

Adelaide, Australia: 14,000 km to come from Suzuka, 20,000 km back to Didcot

Suzuka, Japan: 14,000 km outward trip only

Estoril, Portugal: 5,200 km return trip

Monza, Italy: 2,200 km return trip

Spa, Belgium: 700 km return trip

Budapest, Hungary: 4,000 km return trip

SEE YOU NEXT YEAR

Two hours after the winner has crossed the finish line, the circuit is practically empty. All that remain are the occasional scraps of litter, traces of rubber on the track, and a group of journalists busy finishing their articles in the press office. Drivers and spectators are all long gone as the last trucks, having loaded all their equipment, pull out of the paddock. There is always a tinge of sadness when the curtain falls on another Grand Prix. However, Formula 1 will be back. In a year's time. Until then, the world tour continues, to other countries, to other circuits.

PARTS INSPECTION
Hubs and wishbones are coated with "Ardrox", a red penetrating solution. This is cleaned off and a white solution is applied. If a red line appears, the part is cracked

WHEEL-BEARING CHANGE
The wheel bearings, which are situated between the fixed stub axle and the rotating hub, are replaced after every race

FRESH PAINT
Cars often come back with chipped paintwork caused by gravel thrown up during the race. They are repainted to ensure the smoothest possible flow of air across the body next time out

Life after Formula 1

John Watson

Drivers rarely leave formula 1. In fact it's more often the other way round. Those that choose to pull out at the peak of their careers – like Hawthorn, Stewart, Hunt, Scheckter, Mansell and Prost – tend to be exceptions. More frequently, with age, certain drivers begin by slipping down the grid before turning to alternative forms of motor racing. Indeed, some fifty ex-F1 drivers were racing in other types of competition in 1993. But what of those who have stopped altogether? About twenty or so have taken up TV commentary, whilst others have earned enough money from the sport to retire on their takings. Others move into totally new fields. Carlos Reutemann, today Governor of Argentina's Santa Fe province, is tipped by some as a future President of the South American republic.

Gérard Larrousse

TEAM MANAGERS

At one time, it wasn't rare for F1 drivers to start their own team, either during their career or at the end of it. Some, such as Brabham and McLaren, gave their names to their teams. Others, like Arrows (Oliver) or Eagle (Gurney), were somewhat less assertive. Except for McLaren and Brabham, few have tasted true success, a fact that supports those who claim that a driving career is not an open ticket to team management at a later date. Since Ligier and Oliver lost control of their teams, Gérard Larrousse is the sole driver-constructor still around today.

NUMBER OF GRAND PRIX RACED BY TEAMS FOUNDED BY FORMER F1 DRIVERS

Team	Grand Prix	Driver
McLaren:	394 *	Bruce McLaren
Brabham:	394	Jack Brabham
Ligier:	277*	Guy Ligier
March:	200	Alan Rees
Arrows:	197	Jackie Oliver
Surtees:	117	John Surtees
Larrousse:	110 *	Gérard Larrousse
Fittipaldi:	104	Emerson Fittipaldi
Penske:	30	Roger Penske
Eagle:	25	Dan Gurney
Hill:	10	Graham Hill
Merzario:	10	Arturo Merzario
LEC:	3	David Purley
Bellasi:	2	Silvio Moser
Rebaque:	1	Hector Rebaque
Amon:	1	Chris Amon
Lyncar:	1	John Nicholson

teams still involved in Formula 1

ON THE OTHER SIDE OF THE CAMERA

Twenty or so former F1 drivers still play an active role in today's F1 scene. Gérard Larrousse directs a team, Wilson Fittipaldi manages the career of his son Christian whilst Lauda, Oliver and Edwards respectively hold top positions with Ferrari, Footwork and Lotus. The majority, however, have taken up TV commentary, like Palmer (BBC), Daly (ESPN), Mass (RTL), Watson and Belmondo (Eurosport) and Nakajima (Fuji). Not forgetting a special mention for the late James Hunt who will long be remembered as a master of the art at the BBC.

AT WHAT AGE DO DRIVERS LEAVE FORMULA 1?

30 or less: 4

31-32 years: 5

33-34 years: 7

35-36 years: 7

37-38 years: 8

39-40 years: 6

41-42 years: 3

43-44 years: 3

45 or over: 2

AGE LIMIT

The average retirement age for drivers totalling more than 50 Grand Prix starts is 36. Six of the 1993 grid were over that age – Patrese, Alliot, Warwick, Boutsen, Alboreto and Prost. The latter won his fourth title at the age of 38, whilst Nigel Mansell was 39 when he took the crown in 1992. Clearly, the top drivers age well.

COLLECTOR

Phil Hill has returned to California where he restores classic cars and pianos. His collection forms one of the USA's most celebrated automobile museums.

DEALERSHIP

Juan Manuel Fangio, today in his eighties, still directs the main Mercedes dealership in Buenos Aires. He also serves as ambassador for the German company throughout the world.

BUSINESSMAN

Nelson Piquet owns a number of Pirelli outlets in Brazil. This year saw him take part in the Indianapolis 500 after a serious accident at the same circuit in 1992.

WHERE ARE THEY NOW?

MERCEDES W196
1954 World Champion (Fangio)
Mercedes Museum, Stuttgart

LOTUS 49
1968 World Champion (Hill)
Private collection (Setton), France

FERRARI 312 T2
1975 World Champion (Lauda)
Location unkown

BRABHAM BT52
1983 World Champion (Piquet)
Wheatcroft Museum, Donington

McLAREN MP4/5
1989 World Champion (Prost)
McLaren Collection, Woking

WILLIAMS FW14
1992 World Champion (Mansell)
Williams Collection, Didcot

GOVERNOR
Carlos Reutemann, who once came very close to winning the world F1 title, is making a name for himself in politics. Elected Governor of the Santa Fe Province in Argentina, he could well one day become President of his home country.

FARMER
Chris Amon, one of Formula 1's unlucky heroes, has returned to native New Zealand where he has followed on from his father, a wealthy landowner and sheep rancher.

AIRLINE PILOT
Niki Lauda has created his own airline company, Lauda Air. When his job as consultant with Ferrari leaves him the time, he likes nothing more than taking the controls of one of his Boeings.

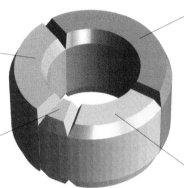

Sports-prototypes:
10 drivers (9%)
Bell, Pescarolo, Lees,
Migault, D. Brabham,
Raphanel, etc

Touring cars: 22 drivers (42%)
Jones, Nannini, Beltoise,
Jarier, Schneider, Moreno,
Capelli, Larini, Bailey, etc

Miscellaneous:
6 drivers (11%)
Lammers, Berg, Schlesser,
Byrne, Naspetti, Borgudd

Formula Indy: 15 drivers (28%)
Andretti, Fittipaldi, Mansell,
Piquet, Danner, Cheever, Gachot,
Johansson, Grouillard, Fabi, etc

STILL RACING
Some fifty former F1 stars still actively compete. Indy racing is a favourite refuge for past F1 drivers, including three ex-World Champions, namely Fittipaldi, Andretti and Mansell. A fourth, Nelson Piquet, swelled their ranks for the 1993 Indy 500. The decline of Sports-prototype racing has plugged one favourite area for re-employment, but the current return to favour of touring cars has provided new opportunities.

INDY RACING
Emerson Fittipaldi, 1993 Indianapolis 500 winner, is a leading light in Indy racing. He also runs "Hugo Boss" shops and owns fruit plantations in Brazil.

MANAGER
Keke Rosberg wears many hats. As well as driving for Opel in touring cars, he commentates for TV and looks after the F1 interests of fellow Finns Lehto and Hakkinen.

INDUSTRY
Jody Scheckter lives in Atlanta where he owns a company selling shooting simulators to the American army and police. Has never returned to his native South Africa.

PUBLIC RELATIONS
Jackie Stewart works in Public Relations, notably for Ford. He also keeps an eye on the career of his son Paul, a driver himself and owner of his own Formula 3000 team.

Index